Tort Law in Japan

Tort Law in Japan

Hiroyuki Kihara

This book was originally published as a monograph in the International Encyclopaedia of Laws/Tort Law.

General Editors: Roger Blanpain, Frank Hendrickx
Volume Editor: Ingrid Boone

Wolters Kluwer
Law & Business

Published by:
Kluwer Law International
PO Box 316
2400 AH Alphen aan den Rijn
The Netherlands
Website: www.kluwerlaw.com

Sold and distributed in North, Central and South America by:
Aspen Publishers, Inc.
7201 McKinney Circle
Frederick, MD 21704
United States of America
Email: customer.service@aspenpublishers.com

Sold and distributed in all other countries by:
Turpin Distribution Services Ltd.
Stratton Business Park
Pegasus Drive, Biggleswade
Bedfordshire SG18 8TQ
United Kingdom
Email: kluwerlaw@turpin-distribution.com

ISBN 978-90-411-6020-1

This title is available on www.kluwerlawonline.com

The Author

Hiroyuki Kihara was born in 1975 in Tokyo, Japan. He received his Bachelor of Laws from Meji Gakuin University in 1997, his Master of Laws in 1999 from Yokohama National University, and his Doctor of Laws in 2004 from Yokohama National University. He worked at the Asia University, Faculty of Law as a Lecturer from 2005 to 2008 and as an Associate Professor of Law from 2008 to present. His major research interests are in the area of contract law, comparative contract law, and tort law. He is a member of the Japan Association of Private Law, the Japan Society of Comparative Law and the Japanese American Society for Legal Studies.

The Author

Table of Contents

Table of Contents

List of Abbreviations

§1. Judgments of the Courts

DCJ	Judgment of the District Court (Chiho-Saibansho Hanketsu)
HCJ	Judgment of the High Court (Koto-Saibansho Hanketsu)
SCJ	Judgment of the Supreme Court (Saiko-Saibansho Hanketsu)
SCJ (FB)	Judgment of the Supreme Court through Full Bench (Saiko-Saibansho Daihotei Hanketsu)
STJ	Judgment of the Supreme Tribunal (Taishinin Hanketsu)

§2. Law Reports

Hanji	Hanrei-jiho (Cases-News Report)
Hanta	Hanrei-taimuzu (Cases-Times)
Hyoron	Hanrei-Hyoron (Cases-Review)
Kamin	Kakyusaibansho Minji-Saibanreishu (Report on civil cases of the lower courts)
Keiroku	Daishinin Keiji-Hanketsuroko (Report on criminal cases of the Supreme Tribunal)
Kinsho	Kinyu-Shoji Hanrei (Financial and commercial cases)
Kominshu	Kotsujiko Minji-Saibanreishu (Report on civil cases of traffic accidents)
Minroku	Taishinin Minji-Hanketsuroko (Report on civil cases of the Supreme Tribunal)
Minshu	Saikosaibansho Minji-Saibanreishu (Report on civil cases of the Supreme Court)
Shimbun	Horitsu-Shimbun (Newsletter for lawyers)
Shumin	Saikosaibansho Saibanshu-Minji (Report on Supreme Court cases – civil cases)

List of Abbreviations

General Introduction

§1. GENERAL BACKGROUND OF THE COUNTRY

I. Geography

1. Japan is composed of 6,852 islands in East Asia. Its four main islands, Honshu, Hokkaido, Kyushu, and Shikoku, accounting for about 97% of the land, are located in between the Pacific Ocean and the Sea of Japan. Since the islands of Japan are widely distributed from north to south, it is the neighbour of five countries, China, South Korea, North Korea, Russia, and Taiwan.

2. This country consists of approximately 378,000 square kilometres of land and water area. According to the 2010 Population Census,[1] the total population of Japan (as of 1 October 2010) is 128.1 million.[2] Tokyo is the capital of Japan, and has a population of approximately 13.1 million.[3] The number of foreign residents living in Japan is 1.6 million (1.3% of the total population). They are Chinese (460,000), Koreans (423,000), Brazilians (153,000), Filipinos (146,000), and others.[4] Most of the population speaks Japanese as their first language.

II. History[5]

A. Early Japan

3. The Japanese archipelago remains unchanged since 10,000 years ago. It is believed that the first human being began to live in Japan a few million years ago

1. Population Census is conducted every five years. Information in English is available at the homepage of the Statistic Bureau, Ministry of Internal Affairs and Communications at <http://www.stat.go.jp/english/data/kokusei/index.htm> (accessed 20 Oct. 2014).
2. See Population and Households of Japan 2010, Ch. I: Size and Geographical Distribution of the Population at <http://www.stat.go.jp/english/data/kokusei/2010/poj/pdf/2010ch01.pdf> (accessed 20 Oct. 2014).
3. *Ibid.*
4. See Population and Households of Japan 2010, Chapter XI: Population of Foreign Residents at <http://www.stat.go.jp/english/data/kokusei/2010/poj/pdf/2010ch11.pdf> (accessed 20 Oct. 2014).
5. For detail of Japanese history in English, see John W. Hall, *Japan From Prehistory to Modern Times* (First Tuttle ed. 1971); Milton W. Meyer, *Japan A Concise History* (4th ed. 2009); Conrad Totman, *A History of Japan* (2005).

from Sakhalin, and then, there was migration from the South Sea Islands and the Korean Peninsula.

4. From c.8,000 BC to c.300 BC was the 'Jomon period'. It lasted for about 8000 years. Jomon period was named after 'rope pattern' carved on the surface of pottery at that time. Jomon people lived on hunting, fishing, and food gathering.

5. From c.300 BC to c.300 AD was the Yayoi Period. It lasted for approximately 600 years. Farming was practiced, iron and bronze were transmitted from the continent. It is thought that the majority of Yayoi people were emigrated from the continent, who began to expel the Jomon people by armour made of iron and bronze.

6. Once rice and precious metals had been transmitted from the continent, 'villages' were built in various places. As the population grew, competition among villages and communities increased, resulting in the domination of the strong over the weak. Statute-based aristocratic system was developed forming the early structure of a 'state'. Stratification of wealth and poverty within the society were created. Around the fourth century, large keyhole-shape tombs known as *kofun*, were constructed by the ruling powers. This era is called 'Kofun period' named after the *kofun* tombs. By the fourth century, the scattered tribes were united under the Yamato Kingship.

B. Construction of the 'Nation' Centred on the Emperor

7. The headquarters of Yamato kingship was placed in Asuka region (located in modern Nara prefecture) from the late sixth century until the early eighth century; this era is called 'Asuka period'. Domestic domination of Yamato kingship was established in the second half of the sixth century. During the middle of seventh century, a centralized government under the ruling of the emperor was completed.

8. In 710, the capital was moved to Heijo-kyo of Nara from the Asuka region. This era is called 'Nara period' and lasted until late eighth century, and was a period of Buddhist influence in Japanese culture. In 794, the capital was moved to Heian-kyo of Kyoto. This era known as 'Heian period' lasted for about 400 years. In the ninth century, the aristocratic Fujiwara family ruled as the real power of politics on behalf of the emperor. The aristocratic central government of Heian period started to face challenges in the tenth century, as provincial and local political entities began to assume greater importance.

C. Era of the Samurai (the Warriors)

9. Since the power of Fujiwara family began to decline in the early eleventh century, the military class became more influential. In the twelfth century, two military families, the Minamoto family (Genji) and the Taira family (Heike) gained more power. Through a struggle of power between the two families, the Minamoto family finally won the battle with the Taira family, and Minamoto Yoritomo opened the shogunate in Kamakura (located in modern Kanagawa prefecture) in 1185 until 1333. This era is called 'Kamakura period' and marked the beginning of the Samurai (the Warriors) era. In the thirteenth century when the Hojo family took over the ruling, the shogunate began to show signs of decline as a result of the Mongol invasion in 1274 and 1281. Eventually Emperor Go-Daigo from Kyoto restored the imperial power and overthrew the Kamakura shogunate.

10. After the termination of Kamakura shogunate ruling, large-scale of civil wars occurred and lasted for about sixty years. Emperor Go-Daigo was defeated by Ashikaga Takauji in 1336, and he appointed himself as a shogun and established his government in Kyoto in 1338. This was the start of the 'Muromachi period', which lasted from 1338 to 1573. However, during the fifteenth and sixteenth centuries, the Muromachi shogunate gradually lost its influence over outer regions and failed to control the warlords who controlled over the different parts of Japan. The civil war called the 'Onin War' began in 1467, and the warlords continued to fight among themselves for a century. This era is called the 'Sengoku (civil war) period'.

11. By the middle of the sixteenth century, Oda Nobunaga, one of the most powerful warlords, conquered many other warlords and embarked on the first step towards unification of Japan by capturing the capital Kyoto and overthrowing the Muromachi shogunate in 1573. His successor, Toyotomi Hideyoshi continued the unification process and finally unified the nation in 1590. Nonetheless, after his death in 1598, Tokugawa Ieyasu took over the power to reign. Tokugawa subdued Toyotomi's loyalists and other rivals in the battle of Sekigahara in 1600, and became the absolute ruler of the country. He was appointed as a shogun and established his shogunte in Edo (presently Tokyo). This era from 1573 to 1603 is called 'Azuchi-Momoyama period'.

12. The Tokugawa shogunate, as a unified government, reign over one quarter of the whole country and subdued the feudal lords in the other parts of the country. Then, the Tokugawa shogunate continued to rule Japan for about 260 years. This era from 1603 to 1868 is called 'Edo period'. During the Edo period, seclusion policy was adopted, where the country was almost completely isolated by forbidding travelling abroad and trading with other countries except China and the Netherland at trading port of Nagasaki. However, in 1853, Commodore Matthew Perry and the 'Black Ship' of the US Navy arrived in Japan and forced the Tokugawa shogunate to open up ports for trading. Eventually, the Tokugawa shogunate was compelled to accept this proposal, and concluded commercial treaties with the United States, England, France, Russia and the Netherland subsequently. These political pressures led to the restoration of sovereign power from the Tokugawa shogunate to the emperor in 1867, which marked the end of the Edo period.

D. Modern Era

13. Emperor Meiji moved from Kyoto to Tokyo which became the new capital of Japan until now, and established the Meiji government in 1868. Emperor Meiji was instituted as the ruling power and he ruled until he died in 1912. This era from 1868 to 1912 is called 'Meiji period'. The new government made attempts to abolish the treaties concluded between the Tokugawa shogunate and the Western countries, which were unequal to Japan in terms of tariff and extraterritoriality jurisdiction. Unequal treaties gave Japan no autonomy to decide the rate of tax concerning imported goods, and no rights to arrest and trial foreigners who committed crimes in Japan. Therefore, in order to regain independence from the Western countries and to conclude new and more equal treaties, it was an urgent task for the Government to establish modern legal systems and to act the Constitution, the Civil Code, the Penal Code and other important codes and statutes. At the same time, the Government started modernization, in order to catch up and mend the gap between Japan and the Western countries economically and militarily. After the victories in the First Sino-Japanese War (1894–1895) and the Russo-Japanese War (1904–1905), Japan gained control of Taiwan, Korea, and the southern half of Sakhalin, and was recognized as one of the major powers in the world.

14. The era from 1912 to 1926 is called 'Taisho period' under the power of Taisho emperor. World War I broke out in 1914. Japan joined the Allied powers and acquired territorial expansion in the East. 'Showa period' under the power of Showa emperor started from 1926. The Great Depression began in 1929. In order to overcome the serious impact in the society, Japan embarked on its expansionist policy abroad. In 1931, Japan occupied Manchuria and built a puppet state of Manchukuo. Japan continued to invade other parts of China, bring to the outbreak of the Second Sino-Japanese War in 1937. This was the precedent of World War II in Asia. When Japan attacked the US Pearl Harbor in 1941, the US retaliated and thus began the war in Asia on a large scale. Japan fought against the Allied Powers in Asia by invading Southeast Asian countries with an aim to build a 'Great East Asia Co-prosperity Sphere'. However, in 1945, Japan agreed to an unconditional surrender to the Allied Powers, and lost all the territory acquired after 1894.

15. After World War II ended, Japan was occupied by the Allied Powers until 1952. Supreme Commander for the Allied Powers (SCAP) occupied Japan with its basic policy of occupation as to demilitarize and democratize Japan. In 1951, Japan signed the San Francisco Peace Treaty with forty-eight nations and ended the state of war that still existed between them. When the treaty came into effect in 1952, it marked the end of SCAP occupation which allows Japan to regain its independence. Japan resumed a place in the world community by becoming a member of the United Nations in 1956. By 1964, Japan was admitted to the OECD marking its status as an advanced country, which it attained through its rapid growth since independence. Showa Period which saw the high economic growth of Japan in post-war years ended in 1989, as Emperor Showa passed away. It was followed by the Heisei Period, which lasts until today.

III. Political System

16. The State government operates under the principle of separation of powers among the legislative, the executive and the judiciary branches, and the mechanism of checks and balances. The Japanese Constitution, which was enacted in 1946, stipulates the structure and authority of each branch.

17. The provisions for legislative branch are stated in Chapter 4 of the Constitution. The legislature (the Diet) shall be the highest organ of state power, and shall be the sole law-making organ of the State (Article 41 of the Constitution). It is consisted of the 'House of Representatives' with 480 members elected to serve four years term, and the 'House of Councilors' with 242 members elected to serve six years term (Articles 42, 43, 45, 46 of the Constitution, Article 4 of the Public Office Election Act). For election, all citizens 20 years old and above have the right to vote and those over 25 years old have the right to be elected (Articles 9 and 10 of the Public Office Election Act). The authority of the Diet is to enact legislation, to pass national budget and to ratify treaties (Articles 59–61 of the Constitution).

18. The provisions for executive branch are stated in Chapter 5 of the Constitution. Executive power shall be vested in the Cabinet (Article 65 of the Constitution), and the Cabinet shall consist of the Prime Minister, who shall be its head, and other Ministers of State, as provided for by law (Article 66 of the Constitution). The Prime Minister shall be designated from among the members of the Diet by a resolution of the Diet (Article 67 of the Constitution), and he shall appoint the Ministers of State, but a majority of their number must be chosen from among the members of the Diet (Article 68 of the Constitution). The main function of the Cabinet is to conduct affairs of state, to manage foreign affairs, to conclude treaties with approval of the Diet, to administer the civil service, to prepare the budget, and present it to the Diet, to enact cabinet orders, and so on (Article 73 of the Constitution).

19. The provisions for judiciary branch are stated in Chapter 6 of the Constitution. For detail of judiciary, see §2 below which explains about the 'Position of Judiciary'.

20. There are also provisions for local self-government in Chapter 8 of the Constitution. Regulations concerning organization and operations of local public entities shall be fixed by law (Article 92 of the Constitution), that is, the Local Autonomy Act enacted in 1947. Japan consists of forty-seven prefectures, and each prefecture includes cities, towns and village, and all of these units are considered as ordinary local public entities (Article 1-3 of the Local Autonomy Act). The local public entities shall establish assemblies as their deliberative organs, and the members of their assemblies are elected by direct popular vote within their several communities (Article 93 of the Constitution). Then, local public entities shall have the right to manage their property, affairs and administration and to enact their own regulations within law (Article 94 of the Constitution).

IV. Economic and Social Values

21. Japan is a developed country and has the third largest economy in the world by nominal Gross Domestic Product (GDP). The nominal GDP in 2013 was estimated at USD 4.902 trillion,[6] with a per capita USD 38,492.[7] As for the GDP by sector, agriculture only accounts for 1.1%, industry for 25.6%, and services for 73.2% in 2013.[8] Japan has one of the world's largest and technologically advanced industries, and its major exports are motor vehicles, ships, electronics, electrical machinery and chemicals. On the other hand, its major imports are fossil fuels, foodstuffs, machinery and equipment, chemicals, textiles, and raw materials.

22. The total number of labour force in August 2014 was 63.63 million,[9] and agriculture occupied 3.9%, industry occupied 26.2%, and services occupied 69.8% of the labour force in 2010.[10] Unemployment rate was 3.5% in August 2014.[11]

§2. Legal Systems

I. Primacy of Legislation and Codification

23. The Constitution is the supreme law of the nation (Article 98(1) of the Constitution). Therefore, no law, ordinance, imperial rescript or other act of government, or part thereof, contrary to the provisions hereof, shall have legal force or validity. Therefore, any comprehensive codes such as the Civil Code, and any statutes are inferior to the Constitution.

24. There is a dispute over the superiority of a treaty with the Constitution. According to Article 98(2) of the Constitution, 'The treaties concluded by Japan and established laws of nations shall be faithfully observed'. However, it has become a majority opinion that the Constitution is superior to a treaty on the ground that the Constitution requiring strict revision procedure cannot be easily abolished by a treaty.

---

6. GDP (current USD), The World Bank, at <http://data.worldbank.org/indicator/NY.GDP.MKTP.CD> (accessed 20 Oct. 2014).
7. GDP per capita (current USD), The World Bank, at <http://data.worldbank.org/indicator/NY.GDP.PCAP.CD> (accessed 20 Oct. 2014).
8. The World Factbook, CIA, at <https://www.cia.gov/library/publications/the-world-factbook/fields/2012.html> (accessed 20 Oct. 2014).
9. Summary of the June 2014 Survey Results, Statistics Bureau, Ministry of Internal Affairs and Communications, at <http://www.stat.go.jp/english/data/roudou/results/month/index.htm#TAB> (accessed 20 Oct. 2014).
10. The World Factbook, CIA, at <https://www.cia.gov/library/publications/the-world-factbook/fields/2048.html> (accessed 20 Oct. 2014).
11. Summary of the August 2014 Survey Results, Statistics Bureau, Ministry of Internal Affairs and Communications, at <http://www.stat.go.jp/english/data/roudou/results/month/index.htm#TAB> (accessed 20 Oct. 2014).

25. Judges are expected to apply and interpret the law in each case, but not to create legal rules of their own. The doctrine of precedent (stare decisis) is not admitted in Japan. The binding force of judgment is limited and only provision referring to this point may be found in Article 4 of the Court Act, which states that 'A conclusion in a judgment of a higher instance court shall bind the lower instance courts with respect to the case concerned.' However, in practice, judgment of the Supreme Court has a strong influence to subsequent judgments, either in the Supreme Court or in the lower courts.

II. Position of the Judiciary

26. Article 76 of the Constitution provides the basic principles of the judiciary:

(1) The whole judicial power is vested in a Supreme Court and in such inferior courts as is established by law.
(2) No extraordinary tribunal shall be established, nor shall any organ or agency of the Executive be given final judicial power.
(3) All judges shall be independent in the exercise of their conscience and shall be bound only by this Constitution and the laws.

27. Then, the Court Act enacted in 1947 shall apply regarding the Supreme Court and the lower courts prescribed in the Constitution of Japan (Article 1 of the Court Act). The lower courts mean High Courts, District Courts, Family Courts, and Summary Courts (Article 2(1) of the Court Act). Therefore, there are only five different types of courts in Japan.

28. The Supreme Court located in the Metropolis of Tokyo, which is the highest Court of final appeals (Articles 6 and 7 of the Court Act). The Supreme Court shall conduct proceedings and give judgments through a 'full bench', which shall be a panel comprised of all fifteen justices, or a 'petty bench', which shall be a penal composed of three or more Judges (Article 9 of the Court Act). In the following cases, petty bench may not give a judicial decision so that such case must be handled by full bench (Article 10 of the Court Act):

(i) Cases in which a determination is to be made on the constitutionality of law, order, rule, or disposition, based on the argument by a party (except the cases where the opinion is the same as that of the judicial decision previously rendered through the full bench in which the constitutionality of act, order, rule, or disposition is recognized).
(ii) Cases other than those referred to in the preceding item when any law, order, rule, or disposition is to be decided as unconstitutional.
(iii) Cases where an opinion concerning interpretation and application of the Constitution or of any other laws and regulations is contrary to that of a judicial decision previously rendered by the Supreme Court.

29. As for the lower courts: (i) 8 High Courts located in Tokyo,[12] Osaka, Nagoya, Hiroshima, Fukuoka, Sendai, Sapporo, and Takamatsu, which are appellate courts. In addition; (ii) 50 District Courts located in one for each prefecture, which have normally the first instance jurisdiction; (iii) 50 Family Courts located in one for each prefecture, which deal with family cases and juvenile cases; and (iv) 438 Summary Courts located in major and medium-sized cities across the country, which deal with civil cases involving small sums of money and minor criminal cases.

III. Distinction between Public and Private Law

30. Public law disciplines the relationship of national organizations and relationship to the nation and the people. The Constitution and administrative law is its representative, further, Penal Code, Code of Criminal Procedure, Code of Civil Procedure, international public law would be included.

31. On the other hand, private law disciplines the relationship of peoples. Civil law and Commercial law is its representative. However, today, as can be seen in the area of social law and economic law, the distinction between public law and private law is hard to put clearly, and therefore, there may be not much practical benefits to emphasize the distinction between public law and private law.

IV. Sources of Private Law in General and of Tort Law in Particular

A. Sources of Law

32. The main source of law in private law is obtained in the Civil Code which is the general law. Provisions relating to tort law have also been placed in the same Code, but as described below, case law and special law play an important role in the development of tort law.

B. General Law: Civil Code

33. The Japanese Civil Code is a comprehensive Code which is composed of five parts. Part I is the General Part which stipulates the basic rules of civil law, covering capacity of natural persons and juridical persons, juristic acts, agency, and prescription. Part II covers property and real security rights. Part III covers the law of rights and obligations, resulting from contract, management of business (Negotiorum Gestio), unjust enrichment and tort. Part IV deals with family relations and Part V prescribes laws on inheritance.

12. It should be noted that the Intellectual Property High Court was established in 2005 as a special branch of Tokyo High Court to deal with intellectual property lawsuits.

34. The present Civil Code was enacted in 1896. It was only after World War II that Part IV and V, which deal with family law and inheritance law respectively, were completely amended, with the aim of democratizing family relationship and promoting gender equality. Part I, II, and III have not been substantially amended since enactment. However, since 2006, serious effort has been made to revise comprehensively some related chapters of Part I and III regarding 'contract law'.

35. The statutory provisions on tort liability are composed of sixteen articles (i.e., Articles 709–724) under Chapter V (Tort) of Part III (Claims) in the Civil Code. These provisions may be classified into three categories.

36. The general requirements for tort liability are stated in Article 709 (Damages in Torts). That is, 'A person who has intentionally or negligently infringed any right of others, or legally protected interest of others, shall be liable to compensate any damages resulting in consequence'. From this provision, four requirements are required to establish tort liability as follows, and each requirement will be discussed in the related chapter of this text:

(i) The tortfeasor should be at fault: i.e., he acted either with intent or negligently.
(ii) Infringement of rights or legally protected interest of others.
(iii) Causation should exist between tortuous act and the loss.
(iv) Loss should have been incurred.

Article 712 (Capacity for Liability) and Article 713 (Capacity for Liability) relates with the capacity, which is another requirement to establish tort liability.

37. The special requirements for tort liability are stated between Articles 714–719. The meaning of 'special' in this context is that those provisions modify the general requirements derived from Article 709 in some respect. Article 714 (Liability of Person Obligated to Supervise a Person without Capacity), Article 715 (Liability of Employers), Article 716 (Liability of Party Ordering Work), Article 717 (Liability of Possessor and Owner of Structure on Land), and Article 718 (Liability of Possessor of Animal) modify the 'fault principle' under Article 709 with some policy. Article 719 (Liability of Joint Tortfeasors) modify the requirement of 'causation' under Article 709.

38. The rest of the provisions are related to the legal effects, including remedies, in case the general or special requirements of tort liability is satisfied, such as, Article 710 (Compensation for Damages Other than Property), Article 711 (Compensation for Damages to Next of Kin), Article 720 (Self-Defence and Aversion of Present Danger), Article 721 (Fetus' Capacity to Hold Rights regarding the Right to Demand Compensation for Damages), Article 722 (Method of Damages and Comparative Negligence), Article 723 (Recovery in Defamation), and Article 724 (Restriction of Period of Right to Demand Compensation for Damages in Tort).

39. The following are the related provisions of torts stated in the Civil Code of Japan:

> Article 709 (Damages in Torts)
> A person who has intentionally or negligently infringed any right of others, or legally protected interest of others, shall be liable to compensate any damages resulting in consequence.
>
> Article 710 (Compensation for Damages Other than Property)
> Persons liable for damages under the provisions of the preceding Article must also compensate for damages other than those to property, regardless of whether the body, liberty or reputation of others have been infringed, or property rights of others have been infringed.
>
> Article 711 (Compensation for Damages to Next of Kin)
> A person who has taken the life of another must compensate for damages to the father, mother, spouse and children of the victim, even in cases where the property rights of the same have not been infringed.
>
> Article 712 (Capacity for Liability)
> In cases where a minor has inflicted damages on others, if the minor does not have sufficient intellectual capacity to appreciate his/her liability for his/her own act, the minor shall not be liable to compensate for that act.
>
> Article 713
> A person who has inflicted damages on others while he/she lacks the capacity to appreciate his/her liability for his/her own act due to mental disability shall not be liable to compensate for the same; provided, however, that this shall not apply if he/she has temporarily invited that condition, intentionally or negligently.
>
> Article 714 (Liability of Person Obligated to Supervise a Person without Capacity)
> (1) In cases where a person without capacity to assume liability is not liable in accordance with the provisions of the preceding two Articles, the person with the legal obligation to supervise the person without capacity to assume liability shall be liable to compensate for damages that the person without capacity to assume liability has inflicted on a third party; provided, however, that this shall not apply if the person who has the obligation to supervise did not fail to perform his/her obligation or if the damages could not have been avoided even if he/she had not failed to perform his/her obligation.
> (2) A person who supervises a person without capacity to assume liability, on behalf of a person who has the obligation to supervise, shall also assume the liability under the preceding paragraph.
>
> Article 715 (Liability of Employers)
> (1) A person who employs others for a certain business shall be liable for damages inflicted on a third party by his/her employees with respect to the execution of that business; provided, however, that this shall not apply if the employer exercised reasonable care in appointing the employee or in

supervising the business, or if the damages could not have been avoided even if he/she had exercised reasonable care.
(2) A person who supervises the business on behalf of the employer shall also assume the liability under the preceding paragraph.
(3) The provisions of the preceding two paragraphs shall not preclude the employer or supervisor from exercising their right to obtain reimbursement against the employee.

Article 716 (Liability of Party Ordering Work)
A party ordering work shall not be liable for the damages a contractor inflicted on a third party with respect to his/her work; provided, however, that this shall not apply if the party ordering work is negligent in his/her order or instructions.

Article 717 (Liability of Possessor and Owner of Structure on Land)
(1) If any defect in the installation or preservation of any structure on land causes damages to others, the possessor of such structure shall be liable to the victims to compensate for those damages; provided, however, that, if the possessor has used necessary care to prevent the damages arising, the owner must compensate for the damages.
(2) The provisions of the preceding paragraph shall apply mutatis mutandis to cases where there is any defect in the planting or support of bamboos and trees.
(3) In the cases of the preceding two paragraphs, if there is another person who is liable for the cause of the damages, the possessor or owner may exercise their right to obtain reimbursement against such person.

Article 718 (Liability of Possessor of Animal)
(1) A possessor of an animal shall be liable to compensate for the damages that the animal has inflicted on others; provided, however, that this shall not apply if he/she managed the animal with reasonable care according to the kind and nature of the animal.
(2) A person who manages the animal on behalf of the possessor shall also assume the liability under the preceding paragraph.

Article 719 (Liability of Joint Tortfeasors)
(1) If more than one person has inflicted damages on others by their joint tortious acts, each of them shall be jointly and severally liable to compensate for those damages. The same shall apply if it cannot be ascertained which of the joint tortfeasors inflicted the damages.
(2) The provisions of the preceding paragraph shall apply to any person who incited or was an accessory to the perpetrator, by deeming him/her to be one of the joint tortfeasors.

Article 720 (Self-Defense and Aversion of Present Danger)
(1) A person who, in response to the tortious act of another, unavoidably commits a harmful act to protect himself/herself, the rights of a third party, or any legally protected interest, shall not be liable for damages; provided, however, that the victim shall not be precluded from claiming damages against the person who committed the tortious act.

(2) The provisions of the preceding paragraph shall apply mutatis mutandis to cases where a Thing belonging to others is damaged to avoid imminent danger arising from that Thing.

Article 721 (Fetus' Capacity to Hold Rights regarding the Right to Demand Compensation for Damages)
An unborn child shall be deemed to have been already born with respect to the right to demand compensation for damages.

Article 722 (Method of Damages and Comparative Negligence)
(1) The provisions of Article 417 shall apply mutatis mutandis to compensation for damages in tort.
(2) If a victim is negligent, the court may determine the amount of compensation by taking that factor into consideration.

Article 723 (Recovery in Defamation)
The court may, at the request of the victim, order a person who defamed others, to effect appropriate measures to restore the reputation of the victim in lieu of, or in addition to, damages.

Article 724 (Restriction of Period of Right to Demand Compensation for Damages in Tort)
The right to demand compensation for damages in tort shall be extinguished by the operation of prescription if it is not exercised by the victim or his/her legal representative within three years from the time when he/she comes to know of the damages and the identity of the perpetrator. The same shall apply when twenty years have elapsed from the time of the tortious act.

C. *Case Law and Special Laws*

40. Tort law has a special characteristic in that they are created based on case law. As compared with contract law or property law, tort law has fewer statutory provisions. This fact indicates that case law plays significantly important roles in the domain of tort law, and the jurisprudence on tort liability has been developed based on case law.

41. Case law also plays significant roles in enactment of a special law. A general tendency shows that, when an unpredictable social issue arises, such issue is addressed in accordance with case law, and then, after case law is generally accepted, they are codified as a special law by the legislative body.

42. For example, in response to the increase in traffic accidents and automobile accidents in the 1950s, the court has attempted to dispute resolution in the tort provisions of the Civil Code primarily, but then, it has led to the enactment of the Automobile Liability Security Act (1955).

43. In 1960s, environmental pollution problem became serious in Japanese society. There were four major environmental pollution cases in this era, such as Itai-itai-byo (Itai-itai disease) case (1971, 1972), Minamata-byo (Minamata disease) case in Niigata(1971), Yokkaichi Zensoku (Asthma) case (1972), and Minamata-byo (Minamata disease) case in Kumamoto (1973). These cases led to the enactment of the Air Pollution Control Act (1968), the Water Pollution Control Act (1971), and the Act on Liability for Oil Pollution Damage (1975).

44. In the late 1970s, the problem of so-called defective product has begun to be noticed. Even for this problem, the court had to deal with the provisions of the Civil Code (tort law) first, but eventually, it come to fruition in the enactment of the Product Liability Act (1994).

45. In addition, as an important special law associated with tort include the Act on Liability for Fire Caused by Negligence (1899), the Unfair Competition Prevention Act (1934), the State Redress Act (1947), and so on.

§3. Function of the Law of Torts

46. In general, tort law has multiple functions in society. First, tort law has a function for recovery of damages suffered by the victim. Normally, because the act of the tortfeasor is the cause of the damage occurs, it is fair for victims to claim the compensation to the tortfeasor, and this is the primary function of tort law in Japan.

47. Second, tort law functions as a penalty or sanction against the injuring party. In the era of criminal law and civil law has not been clearly separated, by imposing same damage victim suffered to the tortfeasor, justice was deemed to be carried out, so that the degree of revenge was also constrained thereby. And at the same time it was expected to make satisfaction to the victim. In modern era, punitive damages can be considered to have such a function, but, not as in the United States, this kind of damage is not available in Japanese tort law. For detail, see Part VI, Chapter 7, §3 below.

48. Third, tort law has a function to prevent or reduce the damages. Because it would be obliged for tortfeasor to compensate for damages suffered by the victim, in order to avoid incurring such obligation, the tortfeasor would be careful to avoid such an act, as a result, such a damage would be prevented.

§4. Relationship between Torts and Criminal Law

49. In Japan, torts which belong to civil liability and criminal law which belongs to criminal liability are now clearly distinguished. In the past, there was a 'incidental civil-appeal' (*Futai-Shiso*) following the 'action civile' recognized in French law, the system for the victim to be able to claim compensation against the criminal defendant in criminal proceedings was allowed, but the existing Code of Criminal Procedure enacted in 1948 has been abolished this system.

50. However, according to Article 12 (Support with regard to Claims for Damages, etc.) on the Basic Act on Crime Victims enacted in 2004, it is stated that:

> The State and Local governments shall take such necessary measures as helping Crime Victims claim for damages and expanding the system for organic linkage between the claims for damages and criminal procedures concerning the harm, in order to realize claims for damages caused by Crimes in a proper and smooth way'.

Therefore, as a new tendency from the viewpoint of protecting crime victims, there is a new policy to adjust these two different laws, or two different liabilities.

51. Under the current system distinguishing these two liabilities, there are cases where criminal liability is not established when tort liability is established. For example, infringement of any rights of others may establish tort liability, but it does not mean that it has to establish criminal charges automatically. On the contrary, there are cases where only criminal liability arises and no room to apply tort liability, for example, in case of attempt of crime.

§5. RELATIONSHIP BETWEEN CONTRACTUAL AND DELICTUAL OR TORTIOUS RESPONSIBILITY

I. Situations Where Both Responsibilities Coexist

52. There are some situations where both contractual and tortious liability coexist. For example, the patient may sue a doctor for malpractice and choose to claim compensation either by reason of breach of medical contract between them or by reason of infringement of his right (life, body) under tort law.

53. Another example will be found in the accidents in hazardous workplace. If a employee has an accident at such a workplace, he may claim compensation based on the tort liability of employer, or, he may claim compensation against employer based on the breach of 'considerate obligation to the safety of employees (*Anzen-Hairyo-Gimu*)', which derived from 'good faith' principle (Article 1(2) of the Civil Code), and considered as an incidental or secondary obligation in side of employer under case law.[13]

54. The issue of 'precontracual liability' also lets us consider the relationship between the tort and contract liabilities. At the stage of contract negotiations, if one party breaks off the negotiation without any good reason, and as a result, the other

13. See, e.g., SCJ 25 Feb. 1975 Minshu 29-2-143; SCJ 18 Dec. 1980 Minshu 34-7-888; SCJ 10 Apr. 1984 Minshu 38-6-557. Cf. SCJ 16 Feb. 1981 Minshu 35-1-56; SCJ 27 May 1983 Minshu 37-4-477.

party has suffered a loss, how should we constitute such a liability? Courts and academics have been discussed this issue for many years, and there are several way of thinking, such as considering it as a contractual or quasi- contractual liability, as a tort liability, or as a breach of duty on the basis of a good faith.[14]

55. In addition, both contractual and tortious liability may coexist in the issue of 'professional liability'. For detail, see Part I, Chapter 2, §1 below.

II. Differences of Both Responsibilities

56. According to the Civil Procedure law in Japan, in the case of concurrence of claims, the choice of claim be left to the discretion of the litigants. However, even in such a situation, it is necessary to consider the differences of requirements and legal effects of claims for compensation between tort and contract law.

57. First, there is a difference in the burdens of proof. In tort case, the burdens of proof that the tortfeasor acted negligently or with intent lies with the plaintiff (victim side). However, the burden of proof that there was no fault in breaching contract lies with the defendant (breaching party).

58. Second, there is a difference in comparative negligence. In both tort law and contract law, there are explicit provisions of comparative negligence in the Civil Code. However, in case of breach of contract, the court shall determine the 'liability for damages' and the 'amount thereof' by considering the creditor's negligence (Article 418), but in case of tort, the court shall determine only the 'amount of compensation' by considering the victim's negligence (Article 722(2)). For detail, see Part VI, Chapter 2, §7 below.

59. Third, there is a difference in restriction of period of right to demand compensation for damages. A claim for compensation in contract shall be extinguished if not exercised for ten years (Article 167(1)). A claim for compensation in tort shall be extinguished if not exercised for three years (Article 724). For detail, see Part IV, Chapter 1 below.

60. Fourth, there is a difference in claim for *solatium*. In tort case, compensation for damages to next of kin, that is, claim for *solatium* to the non-pecuniary damage, is allowed under Article 711 of the Civil Code, but such a claim is rejected in a claim for compensation in contract.[15]

61. Fifth, there is a difference in occurrence time of delay damages. Occurrence time of delay damages in tort shall be considered at the time of the tortious act. However, that in contract shall be considered at the time the creditor's request for claim according to Article 412(3) of the Civil Code.

14. See, e.g., SCJ 18 Sep. 1984 Hanji 1137-51; Kyoto DCJ 20 Feb. 1986 Kinsho 742-25.
15. SCJ 18 Dec. 1980 Minshu 34-7-888.

62. Finally, there is a difference in the treatment of attorney's fee. That is, attorney's fee has been considered as damage in tort cases,[16] but not in contract cases.[17]

§6. Protected Interests

63. According to Article 709 of the Civil Code, tort liability would be established if there is an infringement of 'any right of others', or 'legally protected interest of others'. Therefore, the scope of the 'protected interests' is widely open under Article 709, and any specific rule and discipline for each interest has been considered and determined by case law. It is difficult to list all kinds of 'protected interests' allowed in case law comprehensively, but the main categories and the primary types of 'protected interests' are referred to as follows.

I. Property Rights

64. Part II of the Civil Code covers 'property rights' (rights of possession, ownership, superficies, emphyteusis, servitudes, and common) and 'real security rights' (right of retention, preferential rights, rights of pledge and mortgage). Infringement of such rights will establish tort liability. As for the right of possession, there are specific provisions for claiming compensation of damages in Articles 198–200, but, according to the majority opinions in academics, such claims will be established when the requirements of Article 709 are satisfied.

65. There are other property rights covered under special laws other than the Civil Code, such as 'mining right', 'fishery right', 'quarrying right', or, property rights under customary law, such as 'spa right' or 'water right'. Infringement against such rights will also establish tort liability.

66. Intellectual property, such as 'patent right' and 'copyright', is considered as a quasi-property. In case there is an infringement against such a right, tort liability may be established under the Civil Code, but there are also specific provisions for compensation of damage in their related special laws (e.g., Article 102 of the Patent Act, Article 114 of the Copyright Act).

II. Rights or Interests Resulting from Contract or Other Business Transaction

67. Part III of the Civil Code covers the law of rights and obligations, resulting from contract, management of business (Negotiorum Gestio), unjust enrichment and tort. Then, there is an issue whether an infringement against contractual rights by

16. SCJ 27 Feb. 1969 Minshu 23-2-441.
17. STJ 19 May 1915 Minroku 21-725, SCJ 11 Oct. 1973 Hanji 723-44.

third party may establish tort liability or not. Case law allows to establish tort liability in such a case. For detail, see Part I, Chapter 1, §5 below.

68. Recently, infringement against interests resulting from several kinds of business transaction which establishes tort liability has been reported in case law and discussed among academic. For example, in this category, following issues are included: breach of duty to negotiate in good faith, breach of duty to explain, investigate or provide information on the side of business person to consumer, the dealing with fraud, unfair competition, and so on.

III. Rights or Interests Relating to Family Relationship

69. Part IV of the Civil Code covers rights and obligations among family relationship, such as those between husband and wife, and those between parent and child. Tort liability will be established in case there are infringements against such rights, but most of the cases are related with the issue of marriage. There are cases where the courts admitted to establish tort liability in case of unfair discard of engagement (promise of marriage),[18] and unfair discard of common-law marriage.[19]

70. During marriage, 'A husband and wife shall live together and provide mutual cooperation and assistance' under Article 752 of the Civil Code. If one of the spouses has not fulfilled a duty to live together, cooperate, and provide mutual assistance, it would establish tort liability, even though there are no related cases at this moment. In divorce, if the divorce is due to culpability of one of the spouse, for reason that the status of the spouse has been compromised, a claim for compensation for *solatium* by the other spouse is possible.[20]

71. In the case where one of the spouses had committed an act of unchastity (adultery) with a third party, the other spouse can make a claim for damages based on tort against the third party.[21] However, the same claim against the third party by the child of the spouses shall be rejected,[22] because there was no sufficient causation between the parent-child relationship and the act of the third party. In addition, there is a case that tort liability for such a third party would not be established, when the marital relationship had already collapsed.[23]

18. SCJ 5 Sep. 1963 Minshu 17-8-942.
19. SCJ 11 Apr. 1958 Minshu 12-5-789.
20. SCJ 21 Feb. 1956 Minshu 10-2-124.
21. SCJ 30 Mar. 1979 Minshu 33-2-303.
22. *Ibid.*
23. SCJ 26 Mar. 1996 Minshu 50-4-993.

IV. Rights or Interests Relating to Person or Personality

72. There are several types of rights and interests in this category. Under the Civil Code, it is stated that tort liability shall be established in case there is an infringement in the life of other (Article 711), or in the body, liberty or reputation of others (Article 710). These are considered as an absolute right relating to person or personality in tort law.

73. However, the scope of rights or interests relating to person or personality is not limited to life, body, liberty and reputation of others. According to the development of case law, the following issues are also considered to establish tort liability by reason of infringement for right or interest to person or personality, such as, right of privacy, incidental interests derived from privacy (e.g., rights of publicity or name), interests to enjoy sunshine, view, landscape or the like, interests to prevent noise, bad smell, wind damage or the like, interests to prevent sexual harassment and so on. For detail of reputation and privacy, see Part I, Chapter 2, §4 below.

Part I. Liability for One's Own Acts

Chapter 1. General Principles

§1. Unlawfulness and Fault

74. According to Article 709 of the Civil Code, to establish a tort liability infringement of 'any right of others', or 'legally protected interest of others' is considered as one of the requirements. The latter term was included when Article 709 was amended in 2004. Therefore, prior to 2004, if we only saw the provision literally, tort liability would be established only when there was an infringement of 'any right of others'. In fact, there was an old Supreme Tribunal case in 1914,[24] which indicated that as long as there was no right explicitly stated in statutes, there was no room to establish tort liability. However, in 1925,[25] another Supreme Tribunal case expanded the interpretation of 'infringement of any right of others' in Article 709 to 'unlawful infringement of legally protected interest of others', and since this case appeared, this wider and flexible interpretation of this provision has been established as a standard in case law until today.

75. Shortly after this case appeared, reasoning to support the validity of this decision appeared from academic side in 1930. That is, 'any right of others' found in provision of the previous Article 709 only indicated a slight surface of 'unlawfulness', which is considered as an essential requirement to establish tort liability, and it is concluded that tort liability shall be established, not because there was an infringement of 'any right of others', but there was an 'unlawful infringement of interest of others'. At this moment, there was a paradigm shift in understanding of this requirement from 'infringement of any right of others' to 'unlawfulness', and this is called the 'theory of illegality' (*Ihousei-Ron*).

76. Based on this theory, to determine the illegality in each of tort cases, 'correlation theory' (*Sokan-Kankei-Setsu*) has been proposed. According to this theory, to determine whether there was an unlawfulness or illegality, both the 'nature of interest' on the side of victim and the 'manner of infringement' on the side of tortfeasor has to be considered correlatively.

24. STJ 4 Jul. 1914 Keiroku 20-1360.
25. STJ 28 Nov. 1925 Minshu 4-670.

77. By the development of case law and contribution of academics, these two theory have become the prevailing view in tort law, and, as described above, the term 'legally protected interest of others' was inserted in the amendment of Article 709 in 2004. Under this new provision, in case there is an infringement of 'any right of others', which will be considered as an absolute right, such as rights of property, life, body and health, if there is a fact of such an infringement, the requirement of unlawfulness or illegality might be deemed to be satisfied. In case there is an infringement of 'legally protected interest of others', the 'correlation theory' might be applied, therefore, both the 'nature of interest' and the 'manner of infringement' have to be considered correlatively to determine the requirement of unlawfulness or illegality.

78. Finally, it is necessary to explain the relationship between 'unlawfulness' and 'fault'. Both are required to establish tort liability under Article 709, and traditionally in nature, the former has been considered as an objective requirement, and, the latter as a subjective requirement. However, hereupon, these two requirements have been overlapped. That is, as for the requirement of 'unlawfulness', it is required to consider the manner of infringement on the side of tortfeasor under 'correlation theory', which get closer to determine the subjective requirement of the 'fault'. As for the requirement of 'fault', it used to be understood as a state of mind of tortfeasor, but now it is a prevailing view to understand it as a breach of 'duty of care', which get closer to determine the objective requirement of 'unlawfulness'. For detail, see §2 and §3 below. Therefore, there are several attempts in academics to reconstruct these two requirements in the direction of unifying these two requirements, but case law and majority of academics still treat these requirements separately.

§2. Concept of Fault

79. In principle, fault (intention and negligence) is a requirement to establish tort liability. Article 709 lists both terms 'intentionally' and 'negligently' in that provision. According to the drafters of Civil Code, 'intention' is a state of mind of tortfeasor, which recognized or should have recognized the result of his act. However, 'negligence' is a state of mind of him, which could have recognized the result of his act but he failed to do so because of his lack of attention. However, case law and majority of academics tend not to consider the difference on the acts whether it was based on intention or negligence, and, in fact, these factors have not been considered and has no effect in determining the scope of damages.

80. The plaintiff, the victim side, shall bear the burden of proof that the tortfeasor acted negligently or with intent. However, case law has attempted to reduce this burden of proof on the side of plaintiff. One of the methods is the 'prima facie presumption' and, once the plaintiff proves the estimated fact indicating the prima facie fault on the side of the tortfeasor, the court would evaluate it as the fact that the fault existed, unless the defendant rebuts this estimation. Another method is the 'presumption in fact' and it allows for plaintiff to submit a fact indicating the tortfeasor's fault based on indirect evidence, and then court will infer another fact from there, unless the defendant rebuts this indirect evidence. These methods are also used in the context of proving causation between the tortious act and the loss. See Part V, §1 below.

81. There are a few exceptional cases where the 'intention' becomes crucial. One is the 'liability for interference with contractual relations'. In such a case, tortfeasor is only liable if he did such an act with intention. For detail, see Part I, Chapter 2, §5 below. Another is related with insurance contract. In practice, insurance company may refuse to pay the amount of insurance in case the act, for example, death, injury or arson, whatever it is the reason to occur insurance has been executed with intention.

82. As for the term 'negligence', it should be noted that the degree of negligence may be considered in some context. There are two derivative terms, that is, 'slight negligence', – which means normal negligence – and 'gross negligence'. For example, Act on Liability for Fire Caused by Negligence (1899) states that, in case of fire Article 709 of Civil Code shall not be applied, unless the person who caused the fire was 'gross' negligence. The purpose of this Act is to reduce such person's liability for fire, because the scope of damages may be extremely wider in case of fire. In general, it is expected for people to prepare fire insurance to recover damages by fire. However, this rule will only be applied in case the person who caused the fire was slight (normal) negligence, not gross negligence.

83. There has been a long debate among academics regarding the concept of 'negligence'. Traditionally, negligence was considered as a 'lack of attention' focusing on the tortfeasor's state of mind (so-called subjective approach). Recently, it is considered as a 'breach of duty' (so-called objective approach), which becomes predominant opinion today.

§3. Duty of Care

84. As noted above, considering 'negligence' objectively as a 'breach of duty' is now majority opinions among academics and case law, especially in cases of environmental pollution, malpractice and product liability, has been developed to clarify the meaning of 'negligence' from this viewpoint.

85. The meaning of 'negligence' has been firstly discussed in the environmental pollution cases. In the *Osaka Arukari* case (1916),[26] considered as a leading case, people who lived near the chemical company sued the company for damages to their

26. STJ 22 Dec. 1916 Minroku 22-2474.

corps by air pollution resulting from the operation of the factory. The Supreme Tribunal stated that, as long as the chemical company had prepared reasonable facilities to avoid damages resulting from the operation of their factory, the company was not liable, because it was not able to recognize 'intention or negligence' of tortfeasor stated in Article 709 of Civil Code in such a situation. Therefore, as long as they fulfil a duty to avoid foreseeable harm, there is no negligence.

86. Environmental pollution problem has become more serious in Japanese society since 1960s, and some related cases has started to indicate the meaning of 'negligence' in relation to the 'duty of care'. For example, in the *Nigata Minamata* case (1971),[27] the court stated that the company has a duty to reduce or suspend the operation of the facilities in case it is not avoidable to cause damages to human health, even though the highly advanced technology was used. Similarly, in the *Kumamoto Minamata* case (1973),[28] the court states that the company has a duty to avoid the result of pollution as long as the company could foresee such a result. Courts tend to impose a higher duty of care on company, and, especially at the latter case, it is evaluated that the ruling was as same as imposing a strict liability on the company.

87. Similar trends to set higher standard of duty of care can also be found in other types of litigation. As medical malpractice litigation, for example, in the *syphilis transfusion* case (1961),[29] the court stated that a doctor has a higher duty of care, and he is required a duty of care to do his best in order to prevent the transfusion of syphilis. In the *Tokyo SMON* case (1978) involving damages from defective products,[30] the court indicated that '"negligence" in Article 709 of the Civil Code means a duty to avoid the result [of harm] in the end, and under specific circumstances, it is required the presence of foreseeability in the assumption that a proper avoidance measures is expected'.

§4. Capacity

88. Tort liability arises under negligence or intention on the side of tortfeasor. As a result, the 'capacity' to recognize the liability is required to tortfeasor. Provisions dealing with 'capacity' are found in Article 712 and Article 713 of the Civil Code.

89. According to the provisions above, the 'minor who has not sufficient capacity to appreciate his/her liability for his/her own act' (Article 712) and the 'person who lacks the capacity to appreciate his/her liability for his/her own act due to mental disability' (Article 713) shall not be liable to his own act. It should be noted that not all minors be exempt from the liability under Article 712. According to case law,

27. Nigata DCJ 29 Sep. 1971 Hanji 642-96.
28. Kumamoto DCJ 20 Mar. 1973 Hanji 696-15.
29. SCJ 16 Feb. 1961 Minshu 15-2-244.
30. Tokyo DCJ 3 Aug. 1978 Hanji 899-289.

'12 years old' is one of the criteria,[31] and this article would not be applied to minors over 12 years to 19 years old.[32]

90. In cases where a person without such capacity is not liable under Articles 712 and 713, the next article will be applied. Article 714(1) states that 'the person with the legal obligation to supervise the person without capacity to assume liability shall be liable to compensate for damages' that the person without such capacity has inflicted on a third party. For a discussion on Article 714, See Part II, Chapter 2 below.

31. STJ 30 Apr. 1917 Minroku 23-715 (applying Art. 712 to the boy who was 12 years and 2 months old).
32. According to Art. 4 (Age of Majority) of the Civil Code, 'the age of majority is reached when a person has reached the age of 20'.

Chapter 2. Specific Cases of Liability

§1. Liability of Professionals

I. In General

91. With the increase of medical malpractice litigation since the 1960s in Japan, the liability of medical practitioner has been focused on in courts, and then, other professional such as legal practitioner and architects has also come to be seen as an issue in case law. However, it is still recent to discuss on the theme of 'professional liability' among academics, and related research on professional liability has just developed since 1990s.

92. There are several features for discussing the professional liability. First, most of the profession takes a license qualification system, and there is a special law for each profession such as the Medical Practitioner's Act, the Attorney Act, the Judicial Scrivener Act, the Certified Public Accountants Act, the Certified Public Tax Accountant Act, and the Architect Act, including provisions of licensing, specific duties, and penalty. Therefore, it is necessary to refer to the disciplines under such special law to understand each profession's liability. Second, while the liability of profession becomes severe, professional liability insurance has been developed by many insurance companies. Insurance system is important not only for the 'recovery of damage' for the victim, but also for the safety net on the side of the profession. Third, this is a situation where both contractual and tortious liability may coexist. For example, in the case of medical malpractice, the patient may claim compensation based on the tort liability or on the reason of the breach of contract by the medical practitioner. The standard of care of professions in contract law and tort law has been discussed as below.

93. In the area of contract law, it is not intended to impose heavy liability on the side of profession because contractual parties are considered in equal position. However, most of the contract in which involves profession as one of the parties is the 'mandate contract' or the 'quasi-mandatory contract' under Articles 643 and 656 of the Civil Code so that the provision of 'Duty of Care of Mandatory' under Article 644 of the Code shall be applied, which provides that 'A mandatary shall assume a duty to administer the mandated business with the care of a good manager compliance with the main purport of the mandate.' The standard of the 'care of a good manager' in this context means that the mandatary (the profession) owes a duty of care from the viewpoint of the 'reasonable person' considering his or her occupation or position. Therefore, contractual liability is established when the profession fails to satisfy such a duty of care. This standard is higher than that of the 'care identical to that he/she exercises for his/her own property' stated in Article 659 of the Code. In addition, in the case of the certain professions' liability, such as architect, the provision of 'contract for work' under Article 632 of the Civil Code may be applied. According to Article 632, 'A contract for work shall become effective when one of the parties promises to complete work and the other party promises to pay remuneration for the outcome of the work'. Therefore, in such a situation, whether the profession had completed work or not becomes a criterion to establish contractual liability.

94. In the area of tort law, fault (intention or negligence) is a general requirement to establish tort liability. Then, as I already explained in Chapter 1 of Part I, the concept of negligence is now considered objectively as a 'breach of duty'. Therefore, whether the profession is liable or not in tort law depends on the type and degree of duty each profession should be owed in the light of his or her occupation and position, and it has been developed by case law. The following discussion is mainly focused on case law determining the duty of care and imposing tort liability on each profession.

II. Medical Practitioners

95. There are two main issues where medical practitioners are liable under tort law, that is, medical malpractice and informed consent.

96. In the case of medical malpractice, courts tend to require higher standard of duty of care. For example, the Supreme Court held that the doctor had a higher duty of care to do his best in order to prevent the transfusion of syphilis to the patient.[33] Medical standards required for the medical practitioner, is of the level being practiced in clinical medicine at the time of the clinic.[34] In addition, even if the doctor follows the medical practice that is common, it cannot be said that it is in accordance with medical standards.[35] Medical standards are determined individually considering the scale and nature of medical institutions.[36] Therefore, the doctor in the core area hospital is obliged to provide advanced medical care,[37] but on the other hand, the doctor in is a small hospital that is in private practice is obliged to transfer immediately the patient there is a possibility of serious illness to the medical institution that can provide advanced medical care there.[38]

97. In the case of informed consent, the doctor, prior to provide the medical practice, has a duty to explain the content and risk of therapeutic intervention for a patient, and the doctor is required to obtain the consent of the patient. The medical practice, which was conducted without the consent of the patient, is evaluated as an unlawful act of infringing the right to self-determination of the patient, and in such a case, the doctor is liable for damages under tort law. In case the patient has refused blood transfusion based on religious convictions, the Supreme Court held that the right to self-determination of the patient has been infringed by the doctor who conducted a blood transfusion, and ordered to pay *solatium* based on tort.[39]

33. SCJ 16 Feb. 1961 Minshu 15-2-244.
34. SCJ 30 Mar. 1982 Hanji 1039-66.
35. SCJ 16 Feb. 1961 Minshu 15-2-244; SCJ 23 Jan. 1996 Minshu 50-1-1.
36. SCJ 9 Jun. 1995 Minshu 49-6-1499.
37. *Ibid.*
38. SCJ 25 Feb. 1997 Hanji 1598-70.
39. SCJ 29 Feb. 2000 Minshu 54-2-582.

III. Legal Practitioners

98. When there is a dispute between attorney and client, such as legal malpractice by attorney, most of the claims for compensation are based on the contract between them on the reason of violation of attorney's breach of duty. It is said that attorney has not only the duty to 'care of a good manager' under Article 644 of the Civil Code, but also the duty to 'perform in good faith' under Article 1(2) of the Attorney Act. However, the claims for compensation under tort law may be found in case there are unlawful acts by attorney, such as unfair lawsuit,[40] injury to reputation,[41] or injury to privacy during the lawsuit against the third party.[42]

99. There are many lawsuits against judicial scrivener, primarily engaged in the practice of registration of real estate. Most of the troubles between judicial scrivener and client are also resolved under contract law or the Judicial Scrivener Act as in the case of above mentioned attorney's case. However, when the third party has suffered damages by the lack of real estate registration procedures by judicial scrivener,[43] he is liable to compensate damages under tort law. There is also a case where the judicial scrivener was complicit in the fraud at the sales contract of real estate on the issue of Genya-Shoho, that is, a selling of worthless land by unscrupulous real estate developers,[44] and the Court held that he is liable under tort law.

IV. Builders and Architects

100. Builders may be liable under contract law in case there is contract for work or mandate contract with client. Builder (contractor) may also be liable under tort law in case he built defective building for client. For detail, see Part II, Chapter 1, §2 below.

101. Architect's professional liability is much more complicated than that of builder. Not only because architect is subject to the Architect Act, but also because their range of work is wide so that it is necessary to consider the legal relations with others separately. Architect may be engaged in design of building, construction and supervision of construction, and in some cases the same architect would undertake all of the work as a representative or an employee of the construction company, and, in other case he would undertake a part of the work as a subcontractor. In the former

40. Tokyo HCJ 16 Jul. 16, 1979 Hanji 945-51; Tokyo DCJ 9 Oct. 1995 Hanji 1575-81; Tokyo DCJ 27 Feb. 1998 Hanta 1028-210.
41. Osaka DCJ 31 Oct. 1983 Hanji 1105-75; Osaka HCJ 26 Feb. 1985 Hanji 1162-73; Kyoto DCJ 18 Jan. 1990 Hanji 1349-121; Tokyo DCJ 8 Jul. 1993 Hanta 824-178; Tokyo HCJ 17 Dec. 1997 Hanji 1639-50.
42. Tokyo HCJ 22 Sep. 1999 Hanta 1037-195.
43. As for the defects on registration documents created, see, e.g., SCJ 28 Nov. 1975 Shumin 116-557. As for the defect on warranty created, see, e.g., Nagoya DCJ 10 Apr. 2000 Hanji 1717-119. As for the defect on topographic map created, see, e.g., Sendai HCJ 26 Feb. 1988 Hanta 663-141.
44. Kobe DCJ 21 Jan. 1997 Hanta 942-164.

cases when the architect undertakes the whole work, the architect as a representative of the company has a contractual relationship with the client so that he shall be liable for damages caused by the defects on design, construction or supervision of building under the contract on the reason of breach of higher duty of care.[45] The architect may also be liable under both contract law and tort law in case he runs an architecture firm privately.[46] When he is liable as an employee in such a case, the employer of the architect is liable on tort against the client or the third party under Article 715 of the Civil Code.[47] For detail of the employer's liability, see Part II, Chapter 1, §1 below. In the latter case when the architect only undertakes a part of the work, he has no contractual relationship with the client and the third party so that he may be liable under tort law for causing damages by defects on his work.[48]

V. Others

102. As well as the professionals have discussed so far, other professionals are liable under contract law based on the contract between professional and client on the reason of violation of professional's breach of higher duty of care, but they may also be liable under tort law. For example, tax accountant is liable under tort law in case he submitted a financial income tax return based on false.[49] Certified Public Accountant (CPA) is liable for any major false statements within the securities report or omission of important information by tort law or by the Financial Instruments and Exchange Act. For detail of this Act, see Part III, Chapter 5, §2 below. Notary is a public officer so that his or her tortious act is subject to the provisions of State Redress Act. For detail of this Act, see §2 below.

§2. Liability of Public Authorities

103. According to Article 17 of the Constitution enacted in 1946, 'Every person may sue for redress as provided by law from the State or a public entity, in case he has suffered damage through illegal act of any public official'. Under this provision, the State Redress Act was enacted in 1947. This Act is only composed of six provisions.

104. Article 1 of the Act provides the liability of the State or public entity in case a public officer who exercises the public authority, in the course of his or her duties, caused damages to others intentionally or negligently. This provision is related with Article 715 of the Civil Code. For detail, see Part II, Chapter 1, §1 below.

45. Fukuoka DCJ 16 Jul. 1986 Hanta 637-155; Tokyo DCJ 25 Dec. 1991 Hanji 1434-90.
46. Osaka DCJ 27 May 1982 Hanta 477-154.
47. As for the claim by client, see, e.g., Osaka DCJ 26 Dec. 1984 Hanta 548-181. As for the claim by third party, see, e.g., Tokyo DCJ 18 Mar. 1976 Hanji 838-66; Osaka DCJ 28 Jun. 1991 Hanji 1400-95.
48. As for the claim by client, see, e.g., Osaka DCJ 2 Nov. 1978 Hanji 934-81. As for the claim by third party, see, e.g., Tokyo DCJ 27 Feb. 1990 Hanta 743-180; Tokyo DCJ 15 Oct. 1997 Hanta 982-229.
49. Sendai HCJ 26 Feb. 1988 Hanta 663-141.

105. Article 2 of the Act provides the liability of the State or public entity in case damages to others caused by a defect in the placement or administration of a road, river, or other public structure. This provision is related with Article 717 of the Civil Code. For detail, see Part II, Chapter 3 below.

106. Article 3(1) of the Act states that:

> In cases where the State or a public entity assumes the responsibility to compensate for losses pursuant to the provisions of the preceding two Articles, when the person responsible for the appointment or supervision of public officers or the installation or administration of public structures differs from the person who bears the costs of the public officer's salary, remuneration, and other costs or the costs of the placement or administration of public structures, the person who bears the costs also shall assume the responsibility to compensate for such losses.

Then, Article 3(2) states that 'In the case referred to in the preceding paragraph, the person who compensates for the losses shall have the right to obtain reimbursement against the person liable for that loss based on internal relationships.'

107. Article 4 of the Act states that 'The State's or a public entity's liability for damages shall, in addition to being pursuant to the preceding three Articles, be pursuant to the provisions of the Civil Code.' Therefore, the general requirements and legal effects of tort law provided in the Civil Code shall be applied in case the State or public entity is liable to others under this Act.

108. Article 5 of the Act states that 'As to the State's or a public entity's liability for damages, if Acts other than the Civil Code provide otherwise, such Acts shall take priority.'

109. Article 6 of the Act states that 'In cases where the victim is a foreign national, this Act shall apply only when a mutual guarantee exists.'

§3. Abuse of Rights

110. According to Article 1(3) of the Civil Code, 'No abuse of rights is permitted'. This is one of the fundamental principles in the Code so that this principle has been applied in tort law as well.

111. The leading case of this provision related with tort law is the Supreme Tribunal case in 1919.[50] The owner of pine with a historical value sued the national railway company for compensation of damages to the pine blighted by the smoke of train. The Supreme Tribunal dismissed the claim of owner by holding that residents of roadside must sustain the train service from the viewpoint of the need of

50. STJ 3 Mar. 1919 Minroku 25-356.

train on social community life, but, in the obiter dictum, it is necessary to exercise any right within a suitable range, and in case someone intentionally or negligently infringed the rights of others in an unreasonable way by exercising his or her right beyond the appropriate range, the tort liability shall be established. This case indicates that abuse of right may establish tort liability.

112. Even today, in the cases where the person who built a building on the basis of his or her ownership, in determining such act may or may not infringe the legally protected interests to enjoy sunshine and ventilation of others,[51] or to enjoy landscape of others,[52] the 'abuse of rights' has been considered as one of the criteria to satisfy the requirement of 'unlawfulness' so as to establish tort liability.

§4. INJURY TO REPUTATION AND PRIVACY

I. Injury to Reputation

113. Under the Civil Code, tort liability shall be established in case there is an infringement in the reputation of others (Article 710). Traditionally, courts have taken a stance that 'reputation' would be assessed objectively so that it means social honour which a person receives from the society for his or her value of personality, such as the character, virtuous conduct, fame, credit or the like, and it does not include his or her subjective evaluation, such as pride and self-esteem.[53] However, there are increasing numbers of cases where the courts hold that such pride or self-esteem shall be protected in recent years.[54]

114. Injury to reputation (defamation) frequently occurs by the media, and the relationship between the 'freedom of press', which is guaranteed by the Constitution (Article 21) becomes a problem here. According to case law, tort liability for defamation shall not be constituted in case: (i) it is the matter of public interest, and (ii) there is a proof that the matter is the truth, or (iii) there is a good reason to believe that the proof of it is the truth.[55]

115. There is an issue whether defamation could be established for the deceased. There is no Supreme Court case, but the lower courts has been admitted the claim for *solatium* from the bereaved family, by considering the defamation to the deceased who had been the model of novel therein as an infringement of protected

51. SCJ 27 Jun. 1972 Minshu 26-5-1067.
52. SCJ 30 Mar. 2006 Minshu 60-3-948.
53. SCJ 18 Dec. 1970 Minshu 24-13-2151.
54. See, e.g., Nagoya DCJ 26 Sep. 1994 Minshu 1525-99; Aomori DCJ 28 Mar. 1995 Hanji 1546-88; Tokyo DCJ 22 Jun. 1999 Hanji 1691-91; Tokyo HCJ 15 Feb. 2001 Hanji 1471-68; SCJ 24 Sep. 2002 Hanji 1802-60.
55. SCJ 9 Sep. 1997 Minshu 51-8-3804.

interest of 'feelings of memorial or piety' of the members of the bereaved family to the deceased.[56]

116. Another issue is whether defamation could be established for judicial person. In case there is defamation, by applying Article 710 of the Civil Code, the main remedy is a compensation of non-pecuniary loss considering the mental suffering of victims who had the injury to his or her reputation. It is difficult to assume mental suffering for judicial person, but the Supreme Court allows the claim for non-pecuniary loss by the judicial person who received defamation, on the grounds that non-pecuniary loss is not limited to mental suffering, but covers any type of intangible losses.[57]

117. As for the remedy in case of defamation, not only the claim for compensation of non-pecuniary loss under Article 710 of the Civil Code, but also the claim to recover the reputation is allowed under Article 723 (Recovery in Defamation) of the Code. It is stated that 'The court may, at the request of the victim, order a person who defamed others, to effect appropriate measures to restore the reputation of the victim in lieu of, or in addition to, damages'. The 'appropriate measures' indicated in above provisions means 'public announcement of apology', and it is usually taken by posting such announcement in the newspaper. It has been discussed that the order to make public announcement of apology by court may be against the 'freedom of thought and conscience', which is guaranteed by Article 19 of the Constitution, but the Supreme Court held that, when the contents of the public announcement of apology just simply confessed the truth of the situation, and as long as it is intended to express an apology, it does not violate Article 19 (freedom of thought and conscience) of the Constitution.[58]

118. Injunctive relief is also important remedy for victims when the defamation is continuing. Case law widely admits injunctive relief in the case of defamation by ordering the pre-injunction or injunction of publication. For detail, see Part VI, Chapter 7, §2 below.

II. Injury to Privacy

119. By the development of case law, infringement for right or interest of privacy is also considered to establish tort liability. The concept of 'privacy' is relatively new and it was approved in the judgment of Tokyo District Court at the trial court case in 1964,[59] then, it has led to the approval in the Supreme Court by considering privacy as one of the protected right relating to person or personality.[60]

56. Tokyo DCJ 19 Jul. 1977 Hanji 857-65; Tokyo HCJ 14 Mar. 1979 Hanji 918-21; Osaka DCJ (Sakai Division) 23 Mar. 1983 Hanji 1071-33.
57. SCJ 28 Jan. 1964 Minshu 18-1-136.
58. SCJ (FB) 4 Jul. 1956 Minshu 10-7-785.
59. Tokyo DCJ 28 Sep. 1964 Kamin 15-9-2317.
60. SCJ 8 Feb. 1994 Minshu 48-2-149. See also, SCJ 12 Sep. 2003 Minshu 57-8-973.

Further, in recent years, the importance of the protection of personal information is to be strongly recognized in society, and the 'Act on the Protection of Personal Information' was enacted in 2003.

120. Privacy means a protected interest not to present private affairs of people to the public. Therefore, in the case of privacy, unlike the case of defamation, even if there was an announcement of matter that is the truth, tort liability can be established as an infringement of privacy.

121. As for the remedy in case of injury to privacy, the claim for compensation of non-pecuniary loss and the claim for injunctive relief, such as pre-injunction or injunction of publication would be allowed, as in the case of defamation. For detail of injunction, see Part VI, Chapter 7, §2 below.

§5. Interference by a Third Person with Contractual Relations

122. In the past, it was considered that it was not possible to establish tort liability in case there in an infringement of contractual rights by third party, because of the 'relative' nature found in contract, that is, contractual rights and obligations only occur between the contractual parties. However, later on, case law allowed the infringement of contractual right by third party shall establish tort liability, because of the reason that no one has not be able to infringe contractual right as well as other rights, as long as the contractual right is one of the rights the law shall protect.[61]

123. In general, tortfeasor is only liable when he 'intentionally', not 'negligently', infringed the contractual rights of others. Contractual relationship is not always clear from outsider therefore, it is required for tortfeasor to recognize such contractual relationship to establish tort liability when he infringed contractual rights of others.

124. There are several types of infringement of contractual rights by third party. 'Double sale of real property' is one of the examples. When there is a double sale of real property, the ownership of real property belongs to person who satisfies the requirement of 'registration' under Article 177 of the Civil Code. Then, according to case law and majority of academic, in case that the second buyer who knew that the real property was sold to the first buyer from the seller, but nevertheless enacted contract with the seller and made the registration, the second buyer who acted in bad faith shall acquire that real property.[62] However, in such a situation, the action of second buyer may be considered as an infringement of contractual relationship between the seller and the first buyer. This issue was discussed in the Supreme Court,[63] but the Court dismissed the claim of damages under tort law by the first

61. STJ 10 Mar. 1915 Keiroku 21-279 STJ 10 Mar. 1915 Keiroku 21-279.
62. See, e.g., STJ 10 Dec. 1921 Minroku 27-2103; SCJ 31 May 1955 Minshu 9-6-774; SCJ 19 Sep. 1957 Minshu 11-9-1574; SCJ 29 Nov. 1960 Minshu 14-13-2869.
63. SCJ 31 May 1955 Minshu 9-6-774.

buyer, indicating that the action in 'bad faith' is not enough to establish tort liability. It is said that the court attempted to maintain a consistency between the theory of property law and that of tort law.

125. There are many conflicts related to this issue in employment contract. Tort liability shall not be established when a retired employee or manager was just simply against the non-competition clause agreed with his or her previous company.[64] However, according to case law,[65] tort liability would be established, in case the retired employee unfairly uses the trade secret of his or her previous owner, in case he or she retired his or her company in order to cause damages to his or her previous company, or in case he or she takes away customers of previous company in the way of departing from the scope of free competition.

126. To the contrary, the company who induced to retire employee in other company and made a headhunting of such employee in the way of departing from the scope of social reasonableness, shall be also liable to compensate damages for the company whom the employee was headhunted.[66] Further, when the employee or manager retired his or her company voluntarily, and established a new company to compete with the previous company, there are cases where the tort liability was imposed on the new company.[67]

127. Also, there are cases where labour disputes, such as strikes or picketing, shall be established tort liability for labour unions to the company when it is considered as illegal one.[68]

128. Inducing to enter contract by third party in the unreasonable or illegal way may also be considered as an infringement of contractual rights of others. In the case where, based on the request from the customer A, the bank B introduced the construction company C in the insolvency who was the borrower of the B, the construction contract was concluded between A and C. Then, A paid the retaining fee to C, which was recovered as a loan by B later, but, after all, C went bankrupt in the middle of construction. The Tokyo District Court held that B was liable for A's damages caused by providing the incorrect information to A and indicated explicitly that such action is considered as an infringement of contractual rights by the third party.[69]

§6. Others

129. There are no other specific issues to explain in this chapter.

---

64. Tokyo DCJ 16 Oct. 1995 Hanta 894-73; Tokyo DCJ 25 Aug. 1993 Hanji 1497-86.
65. Tokyo DCJ 25 Nov. 1994 Hanji 1497-86.
66. Tokyo DCJ 25 Feb. 1993 Hanta 766-247.
67. Osaka DCJ 3 Mar. 1983 Hanji 1084-122; Tokyo DCJ 27 Feb. 1995 Hanji 1542-68.
68. SCJ 2 Oct. 1992 Hanta 813-191; Tokyo DCJ 6 May 1992 Hanta 798-178.
69. Tokyo DCJ 23 Feb. 1995 Hanji 1550-44.

Part II. Liability for Acts of Others

Chapter 1. Vicarious Liability

§1. EMPLOYEE/EMPLOYER

130. The Japanese Civil Code provides 'Liability of Employers' on Article 715. Case law considers it as a vicarious liability on employer, not as a self- or inherent liability on employer. According to Article 715(1), 'A person who employs others for a certain business shall be liable for damages inflicted on a third party by his/her employees with respect to the execution of that business.' Then, according to Article 715(2), 'A person who supervises the business on behalf of the employer shall also assume the liability under the preceding paragraph.'

131. Article 715 imposes strict liability on employer for damages caused to third party by his employees. This is based on the principle of 'recompense liability' (*Hosho-Sekinin*), that is, there is a heavy responsibility on person who has caused damages to other in the course of making profit, must compensate damages from such profit. However, to be precise, there is a proviso to exempt liability on employer if he 'exercised reasonable care in appointing the employee or in supervising the business, or if the damages could not have been avoided even if he/she had exercised reasonable care'. Therefore, it is an 'intermediate liability' for employer, but there is no case law where this proviso was applied in the Supreme Court level and even few in the lower court level.

132. To establish tort liability of employers under this provision, firstly, 'the relationship between employer and employee' is required. Case law tends to consider it as a 'command and order relationship' between two parties in a broad sense, and there were cases applying this requirement even to the relationship between 'older and younger brothers',[70] or between 'boss and crew in gang',[71] which are not the normal relationship of employer and employee in business. Second, such damage has to occur 'with respect to the execution of that business'. Third, to establish

70. SCJ 27 Nov. 1981 Minshu 35-8-1271 (applying Art. 715 in case the older brother A asked his younger brother B to pick him up by A's car, and B caused traffic accident on the way to go home, and, according to the court, there was a 'command and order relationship' between A and B so that A was liable to compensate damages for third party resulting from B's act.).
71. SCJ 12 Nov. 2004 Minshu 58-8-2078 (applying Art. 715 to the boss in gang and imposing liability on him to compensate damages for third party resulting from his crew member.)

tort liability of employer under Article 715, the employee's act has to been satisfied all requirements of general tort liability under Article 709.

133. There is a controversy for the second requirement above. Case law and academic has continued a long debate regarding the criteria or the scope of 'with respect to the execution of that business'. Case law has been established the principle to determine the 'execution of that business' from the appearance (gaikei-riron).[72] This is a way of thinking, when observed objectively the appearance of the acts of employees widely, as long as it is recognized that such acts are within the scope of the 'execution of that business', employers shall be liable for compensate damages therefrom under Article 715.[73] However, there is some criticism to this principle from academic side on the reason that it is too abstract and unclear criteria to determine tort liability under Article 715. In fact, there are similar cases but reached to the opposite conclusion in this respect. One is that car accident caused by employee on the way home by driving a company's own car, and the court determined that this act was within the scope of the 'execution of that business' and admitted the employer's tort liability under Article 715.[74] The other is that car accident caused by the employee during business trip by driving his private car, and the court determined that this act was out of the scope of the 'execution of that business' and denied the employer's tort liability under Article 715.[75]

134. If the requirements above are satisfied, the employer is liable to compensate damages resulting from his employee, but according to Article 715(3), 'The provisions of the preceding two paragraphs shall not preclude the employer or supervisor from exercising their right to obtain reimbursement against the employee.' However, if it may approve to apply this provision widely, the principle of 'vicarious liability' of Article 715 would be impaired so that case law and academic have tried to restrict the application of this provision. Using the provision of 'comparative negligence' under Article 722(2) to restrict the scope of reimbursement in this situation is one of the way of thinking, but one Supreme Court case, applying the 'good faith' principle under Article 1(2), and stated that, from the viewpoint of equitable sharing of damages between employer and employee, the scope of reimbursement against the employee shall be restricted to the reasonable amount.[76]

135. There is a similar provision in the '*State Redress Act* (1947)'. According to Article 1(1), 'When a public officer who exercises the public authority of the State or of a public entity has, in the course of his/her duties, unlawfully inflicted damage on another person intentionally or negligently, the State or public entity shall

72. SCJ 12 Dec. 1955 Minshu 9-14-2047.
73. *Ibid.*
74. SCJ 4 Feb. 1964 Minshu 18-2-252.
75. SCJ 22 Sep. 1977 Minshu 31-5-767.
76. SCJ 8 Jul. 1976 Minshu 30-7-689.

assume the responsibility to compensate therefore.' Then, Article 1(2) states that, 'In the case referred to in the preceding paragraph, when there was intent or gross negligence on the part of the public officer, the State or public entity shall have the right to obtain reimbursement from that public officer.' There are some differences between these provisions and Article 715 of the Civil Code. First, the proviso to exempt liability of the State or public entity is not provided in this Act, and secondly, the right of reimbursement of the State or public entity is not able to be exercised in case the concerned public officer had intent or gross negligence in doing his tortious act.

§2. Independent Contractors

I. Liability of Party Ordering Work

136. There is a provision for liability of party ordering work in Article 716 of the Civil Code. It states that 'A party ordering work shall not be liable for the damages a contractor inflicted on a third party with respect to his/her work; provided, however, that this shall not apply if the party ordering work is negligent in his/her order or instructions.' This is a consequence derived from the nature of 'contracts for work' in Article 632, which states that contractor's obligation is to 'complete work', and he is in position that he is independent of party ordering work. Therefore, in principle, a party ordering work is not liable for the damages resulting from a contractor's act.

II. Liability of Contractor

137. To the contrary, there is no explicit provision to state tort liability of contractors in the Civil Code. Case law, so far, has imposed tort liability mainly based on Article 709 to contractor restrictively, in case he built defective building intentionally, with gross negligence, or in case such defect is deemed to be considered as high unlawfulness.[77] However, in recent years, there are some cases imposing tort liability under Article 709 to contractor who built a defective building, simply because of infringement of 'interest of residence' of purchaser,[78] or simply because such defect had not been satisfied the safety standard.[79]

77. See, e.g., Kobe DCJ 30 May 1988 Hanji 1297-109; Kobe DCJ (Himeji Division) 30 Jan. 1995 Hanji 1531.92; SCJ 14 Nov. 2003 Minshu 57-10-1561; Kobe DCJ 8 Sep. 1997 Hanji 1652-114; Osaka DCJ 27 Sep. 2000 Hanta 1053.137.
78. SCJ 17 Jun. 2010 Minshu 64-4-1197.
79. SCJ 6 Jul. 2007 Minshu 61-5-1769.

§3. LIABILITY OF LEGAL ENTITIES FOR ACTS OF THEIR ORGANS

138. The organs of a legal entity may be liable to compensate for damages arising from the acts of 'representatives' under some special laws,[80] and from the acts of 'employee' under Article 715(1) of the Civil Code, as already discussed. However, the issue here is, whether the organs of a legal entity itself shall be liable for their acts under Article 709 of the Civil Code or not.

139. The majority of academic seems to approve such a way of thinking. The reason for this is when serious damages occurs over a wide range in product liability litigations or environmental pollution litigations, in terms of relief of victims, they consider that it is necessary and reasonable to impose tort liability on the organs of a legal entity itself. In such a case, business activities are recognized as being integral However, some academics are negative to approve this approach, because some theoretical issues are remained to resolve, such as the possibility to determine 'fault' of the organs of a legal entity, and more fundamentally, the possibility to evaluate tortious 'acts' of the organs of a legal entity.

140. There is no case law in the Supreme Court level indicating this issue, but in the lower court level, there are both positive and negative cases whether to impose tort liability to the organs of a legal entity under Article 709 of the Civil Code.[81]

80. Article 78 (Liability to Compensate for Damages Arising from the Acts of Representatives) of the Act on General Incorporated Associations and General Incorporated Foundations (2006) states that 'A general incorporated association shall be liable to provide compensation for damages caused to a third party by its representative director or other representatives in the course of performing their duties'. Article 350 (Liability for Damages Caused by Acts of Directors) of the Companies Act (2006) states that 'A Stock Company shall be liable for damage caused to third parties by its Representative Directors or other representatives during the course of the performance of their duties'.

81. As for positive cases, see, e.g., Kumamoto DCJ 20 Mar. 1973 Hanji 696-15; Fukuoka DCJ 5 Oct. 1977 Hanji 866-21; Kumamoto DCJ 28 Mar. 1979 Hanji 927-15. As for negative cases, see, e.g., Tokyo DCJ 1 Feb. 1982 Hanji 1044-19; Tokyo DCJ 18 May 1987 Hanji 1231-3; Tokyo HCJ 11 Mar. 1988 Hanji 1271-3; Osaka DCJ 29 Mar. 1999 Hanji 1688-3.

Chapter 2. Liability of Parents, Teachers & Instructors

141. As already mentioned in §4, Chapter 1 of Part I, 'minor who has not sufficient capacity to appreciate his/her liability for his/her own act' (Article 712) and the 'person who lacks the capacity to appreciate his/her liability for his/her own act due to mental disability' (Article 713) shall not be liable to his own act. In such a case, according to Article 714(1), 'the person with the legal obligation to supervise the person without capacity to assume liability shall be liable to compensate for damages' that the person without such capacity has inflicted on a third party. In general, 'person who has parental authority' (Article 818), 'guardian of a minor' (Articles 839–847), 'a guardian of an adult' (Article 8), 'child welfare facilities', etc. can be mentioned in the person who is obliged to supervise those minor or insane person under Article 714(1).

142. According to Article 714(2), 'A person who supervises a person without capacity to assume liability, on behalf of a person who has the obligation to supervise, shall also assume the liability under the preceding paragraph.' That deputy supervisor is obliged to supervise minors or insane person in accordance with the provisions of law or the contract with the supervisor in Article 714(1), and 'teacher of kindergarten and elementary school', 'child minder (baby-sitter)', 'doctor of mental hospital', etc. can be mentioned in such a person.

143. There is a 'proviso' to exempt liability on supervisor in Article 714(1), that is, in case that the person who has the obligation to supervise did not fail to perform his/her obligation, or in case that the damages could not have been avoided even if he/she had not failed to perform his/her obligation. This proviso shall be also applied to deputy supervisor in Article 714(2).

144. To establish tort liability against supervisor or deputy supervisor under Article 714, it is required that the act of tortfeasor (minor or insane person) must have an illegality of unlawfulness. In one case,[82] the Supreme Court states that father is not liable for his 7 years old daughter's act breaking her friend's bone during playing tag, because such an infringement resulting from 'acts of game' should be justified.

145. There is an issue whether the '*Act on Liability for Fire Caused by Negligence* (1899)' shall be applied in case the minor covered under Article 712 caused the fire. It states that, Article 709 of Civil Code shall not be applied in case of fire, unless the person who caused the fire was 'gross' negligence. The Supreme Court stands in a position to apply this Act.[83] Then, the determination of 'gross negligence' as referred to in the Act, has to be considered for supervisor's duty of minors, and, when there was no gross negligence on the supervisor's duty, it is assumed to exempt the liability to compensate for damages caused by the fire.

82. SCJ 27 Feb. 1962 Minshu 16-2-407.
83. SCJ 24 Jan. 1995 Minshu 49-1-25.

146. Article 712 would not be applied to minors over 12 years to 19 years old, because they are considered to have sufficient capacity to appreciate his/her liability for his/her own act. Therefore, such a minor is liable for tort under Article 709 in case he infringed any right of others, or legally protected interests of others. However, from the viewpoint of primary function of tort law, that is, 'recovery of damages', to allow a claim for damages against such a minor will not solve the problem, because, in most cases, such a minor does not have sufficient financial resources to compensate. To solve this issue, the Supreme Court states that, if there is a causal relationship between the 'infringement of such a minor' and the 'violation of the breach of duty the supervisor's obligation imposed on themselves', the supervisor's own tort liability based on Article 709 shall be established.[84]

84. SCJ 22 Mar. 1974 Minshu 28-2-347.

Chapter 3. Liability for Things and Animals

I. Liability for Things

147. According to Article 717(1) of the Civil Code, 'If any defect in the installation or preservation of any structure on land causes damages to others', primarily 'the possessor of such structure shall be liable to the victims to compensate for those damages' and, secondly, 'if the possessor has used necessary care to prevent the damages arising, the owner must compensate for the damages'. According to Article 717(2), 'the provisions of the preceding paragraph shall apply mutatis mutandis to cases where there is any defect in the planting or support of bamboos and trees'.

148. Article 717(1) imposes strict liability on both possessor and owner of such structure. This is based on the principle of 'risk liability' (*Kiken-Sekinin*), that is, there is a heavy responsibility on the possessor and owner of the dangerous goods. However, to be precise, as for possessor, there is a proviso to exempt liability in case he 'has used necessary care to prevent the damages arising', so that, it is an 'intermediate liability' for possessor of such structure.

149. To establish tort liability for things under this provision, firstly, it has to be 'any structure on land'. Therefore, equipment that has been subjected to the land as a building, fence, elevator, escalator, drainage pipe or the like is included. There is a case that security equipment such as alarms and circuit breaker in railroad cross are also included in this.[85] Personal property is not included. Second, it has to be 'any defect in the installation or preservation', and if the structure had not been satisfied the safety standard, it is considered as a defect in case law.[86] In addition, even a huge budget is required to prevent accidents, it would not be a reason for denying the existence of defect.[87] Third, it has to be a causal relationship between the 'defect of such structure' and 'damages', and a victim (plaintiff) side shall owe the burden of proof.

150. If the requirements above are satisfied, the possessor or owner of such structure is liable to compensate damages resulting from defect of such structure, but, according to Article 717(3), 'if there is another person who is liable for the cause of the damages, the possessor or owner may exercise their right to obtain reimbursement against such person'.

151. There is a similar provision in the '*State Redress Act* (1947)'. According to Article 2(1), 'When damage to another person is caused because of a defect in the placement or administration of a road, river, or other public structure, the State or public entity shall assume the responsibility to compensate therefore.' Then, Article 2(2) states that, 'In the case referred to in the preceding paragraph, if there is another person who should assume responsibility for the cause of the damage, the State or

85. SCJ 23 Apr. 1971 Minshu 25-3-351.
86. *Ibid.*
87. SCJ 8 Nov. 1962 Minshu 16-11-2216.

public entity shall have the right to obtain reimbursement therefrom.' Most of the explanations mentioned in Article 717 of the Civil Code also apply to Article 2 of this Act. There are many reported cases which impose liability for State or public entity to compensate damages resulting from a defect in a road,[88] river,[89] or other public structure.[90]

II. Liability for Animals

152. According to Article 718(1) of the Civil Code, 'a possessor of an animal' shall be liable to compensate for damages that the animal has inflicted on others. Then, Article 718(2) states that 'A person who manages the animal on behalf of the possessor shall also assume the liability under the preceding paragraph.'

153. This provision imposes strict liability on possessor or manager of the animal. However, there is a proviso in Article 718(1) to exempt liability in case he or she 'managed the animal with reasonable care according to the kind and nature of the animal'. Therefore, the nature of liability in Article 718 is an 'intermediate liability'.

154. There is no limitation in the scope of 'animal' in these provisions so that any types of animals, such as domestic animals, wild animals and pets shall be included, and majority of academic also include even 'pathogenic bacteria' and 'viruses' in the scope.

155. Who is considered as a 'possessor of an animal' in Article 718(1)? According to Article 180, 'Possessory rights shall be acquired by holding Thing with an intention to do so on one's own behalf'. 'Holding Thing' has to be in independent. Therefore, normally, owner of animal, who is a 'direct possessor' of an animal, is considered as a possessor in this provision. The owner's family member or employee does not hold animal independently, so they are just considered as an 'assistant of possessor', who is not liable under this provision. If there is an infringement to others by animal in such a case, the owner of the animal shall be liable as a possessor under this provision.[91]

88. For defects on road, see, e.g., SCJ 4 Sep. 1962 Minshu 16-9-1834; SCJ 16 Apr. 1965 Hanji 405-9; SCJ 20 Aug. 1970 Minshu 24-9-1268; Sapporo HCJ 18 Feb. 1972 Hanji 659-22; Nagoya HCJ 20 Nov. 1974 Hanji 761-18; SCJ 25 Jul. 1975 Minshu 29-6-1136. For a defect on signal, see, e.g., SCJ 16 Feb. 1973 Minshu 27-1-99; SCJ 13 Mar. 1980 Hanji 968-46.

89. For defects on embankment, see, e.g., SCJ 26 Jan. 1984 Minshu 38-2-53; SCJ 13 Dec. 1990 Minshu 44-9-1186.

90. For a defect on airport, see, e.g., SCJ (FB) 16 Dec. 1981 Minshu 35-10-1369. For a defect on reclaimed land, see, e.g., SCJ 11 Sep. 1980 Hanji 984.65. For a defect on a platform of a railway station, see, e.g., SCJ 25 Mar. 1986 Minshu 40-2-472.

91. SCJ 1 Feb. 1962 Minshu 16-2-143.

156. 'The manager of animal on behalf of the possessor' in Article 718(2) is normally a carrier or bailee under contract, who is considered as an 'indirect possessor'. Then, in case such a manager hold animal independently, he may consider as a possessor in Article 718(1). In this respect, there is some difficulty to understand the relationship between the 'possessor' and the 'manager' of animal in the provisions above.

Part III. Forms of Strict Liability

Chapter 1. Road and Traffic Accidents

157. In the 1950s, the number of automobiles increased, which resulted in a growing number of accidents. The Automobile Liability Security Act was enacted in 1955, which provides for liability for automobile accidents and introduced an insurance system for remedy of the victims. It should be noted that this Act only covers compensation for damages to 'personal injury and death' and other damages would be covered by the Civil Code (Article 709 or 715). Also, method of assessing damages covered by this Act shall be based on that of the Civil Code. The primary provision for 'Automobile liability' is provided under Article 3 of the Act as follows:

> Article 3 (Automobile Liability)
> If a person operating an automobile for his/her benefit causes the death of or bodily injury to any other person through such operation, such person shall be liable to compensate for damage to the victim. However, he/she shall not be liable if he/she proves that neither he/she nor the driver failed to exercise due diligence in operating the automobile and that there was an intention or negligence on the part of the victim or a third party other than the driver and that there was no structural defect or functional disorder in the automobile.

158. The main clause of Article 3 provides that automobile operators, in principle, are held liable for damage arising from the operation of the automobile, however, the proviso to the main clause leaves room for exemption of liability. In this sense, this article provides for liability situated between fault liability and strict liability, like employer's liability. However, this proviso imposes a strict requirement for exemption of liability and provides that the automobile operator is in no event released from his/her liability unless he/she establishes the fulfilment of all three requirements.[92] So, this provision substantially provides for liability which has proximity to strict liability.

159. 'A person operating an automobile' means the person to whom 'operating benefit' (i.e., some kind of benefit from operation of automobile) and 'control over operation' (i.e., influence on operation of automobile) belongs to.[93] The criteria for

92. See, e.g., SCJ 19 Nov. 1971 Minshu 25-8-1236 (court rejected to apply the proviso of Art. 3).
93. SCJ 24 Sep. 1968 Hanji 539-40.

a decision as to whether the person falls under the category of the 'A person operating an automobile' should be inferred from the court precedents. For example, the person who leased the automobile to another person (including a rent-a-car company) falls under the category,[94] but the person who possessed the automobile but had the automobile stolen does not fall under the category.[95]

160. The automobile operator is held liable when he/she causes the death of or bodily injury to any 'other person' (Article 3). Therefore, the automobile operator is not held liable under this provision when the automobile operator himself/herself or any party deemed identical thereto dies or suffers bodily injury.[96] Therefore, who shall be deemed as 'other person' becomes an issue. According to case law, any persons other than automobile operators and drivers are included within the scope of 'other person',[97] even the 'wife' of the automobile operator.[98]

161. Article 5 is the substantive provision of the compulsory insurance (mutual aid) system. This article requires that a contract for automobile liability insurance or a contract for automobile liability mutual aid be concluded for all automobiles to be operated. A person who has committed a breach of this article is subject to penal servitude for a period not exceeding one year, or a fine not exceeding JPY 500,000 (Articles 86-3 and 90 of this Act):

> Article 5 (Compulsory conclusion of contract for liability insurance or liability mutual aid)
> No automobile shall be operated unless a contract for automobile liability insurance (hereinafter referred to as 'liability insurance') or a contract for automobile liability mutual aid (hereinafter referred to as 'liability mutual aid') as provided in this Law has been concluded.

162. Under the compulsory insurance system, the insurance company pays insurance benefits to the victim of a traffic accident. However, the condition precedent to the payment of such insurance benefits is that the victim shall have the right to claim compensation of damages against the automobile operator who is the injuring party (See Article 16(1)). In addition, in case where the insured who is the injuring party has already compensated the victim for damages, the insurance company shall be exempted from its obligation to make payment to the extent of the amount indemnified by it (See Article 16(2)):

> Article 16 (Claim for the amount of compensation for damage against the insurance company)
> 1. If the owner has become liable to compensate for damage pursuant to the provision of Article 3, the victim may, as provided in the Cabinet Ordinance,

94. SCJ 9 Nov. 1971 Minshu 25-8-1160. Compare SCJ 4 Dec. 1964 Minshu 18-10-2043.
95. SCJ 20 Dec. 1973 Minshu 27-11-1611.
96. SCJ 14 Dec. 1962 Minshu 16-12-2407; SCJ 28 Mar. 1969 Minshu 23-3-680.
97. SCJ 29 Sep. 1967 Hanji 497-41.
98. SCJ 30 May 1972 Minshu 26-4-898.

make a claim for the amount of compensation for damage against the insurance company to the extent of the limit of insurance.
2. In the case where the insured has compensated the victim for damage, if the insurance company has indemnified the insured for such damage, such insurance company shall, to the extent of the amount indemnified by it, be exempted from its obligation to make payment under the preceding paragraph.
3. If the insurance company has paid the victim the amount of compensation for damage pursuant to the provision of paragraph 1, such insurance company shall be deemed to have indemnified the insured for his/her damage under the liability insurance contract, except for the case where the damage was caused by malicious intent of the policyholder or the insured.
4. In the case where the damage was caused by the malicious intent of the policyholder or the insured, if the insurance company has paid the victim the amount of compensation for damage pursuant to the provision of paragraph 1, such insurance company may make a claim for reparation for the amount of damage paid by it to the government.

163. In the end, it may be useful to refer to the relationship between compulsory insurance and voluntary insurance. Compulsory insurance does not cover all damages. Under the compulsory insurance system, the insurer predetermines the cap amount of insurance benefits payable upon the occurrence of a traffic accident. For instance, it only covers JPY 30 million for the death of a single person; JPY 750,000 to JPY 40 million (depending on the grade of injury) for a person suffering permanent injury; and JPY 1,200,000 for a person suffering damages due to injury (Article 2 of the Enforcement Ordinance of the Automobile Liability Security Law). Therefore, voluntary insurance covers the shortfall, if the damages in an accident resulting in injury or death are not sufficiently covered by the mandatory insurance. As the standard amount of damages awarded by the court and the reasonable amount of out-of-court settlement are trending upward, voluntary insurance plays a very important role.

Chapter 2. Product Liability

164. Up to the present from the late 1970s, the problem of so-called defective product has become serious in Japanese society. Courts has attempted to resolve such disputes by applying tort liability or contractual liability in the Civil Code first, but finally, the Product Liability Act was enacted in 1994, which provides strict liability for manufactures or related persons who delivered defective products.

165. Prior to the enactment of the Product Liability Act, the Civil Code was the main source to provide remedies for victims who suffered losses from the defective products, but there are certain obstacles for victims to claim compensation for losses caused from the defective product, either based on contractual liability or on tort liability.

In claiming contractual liability under the Civil Code, victim as a plaintiff may claim damages by applying Article 415 (Damages due to Default) or 570 (Seller's Warranty against Defects) of the Code, but the extended damages such as personal injury or death caused by defective product shall not be covered by these provisions in general, and such claim is only available to whom had contractual relationship with purchaser, that is, to the seller who sold the defective product, but not to the manufacturer who made the cause of defective product.

In claiming tort liability under the Civil Code, victim may claim damages directly against the manufacturer by applying Article 709 of the Code, but the general principle of tort law shall be applied in such case, therefore, plaintiff owes the burdens of proof, both that the tortfeasor (manufacturer) acted negligently or with intent and that there was a causal relationship between the tortious act and the loss. Proof of negligence or causation is a heavy burden for plaintiff so that it may lead to result the failure of such proofs.

166. The Product Liability Act was enacted to remove such obstacles, especially found in tort law of the Civil Code. This Act is only composed of six provisions as follows:

> Article 1 (Purpose)
> The purpose of this Act is to protect the victim of the injury to life, body, or property which is caused by a defect in the product by setting forth liability of the manufacturer, etc. for damages, and thereby to contribute to the stabilization and improvement of the life of the citizens and to the sound development of the national economy.
>
> Article 2 (Definitions)
> (1) The term 'product' as used in this Act shall mean movable which is manufactured or processed.
> (2) The term 'defect' as used in this Act shall mean a lack of safety that the product ordinarily should provide, taking into account the nature of the product, the ordinarily foreseeable manner of use of the product, the time when the manufacturer, etc. delivered the product, and other circumstances concerning the product.

(3) The term 'manufacturer, etc'. as used in this Act shall mean the following:
(i) any person who manufactured, processed, or imported the product in the course of trade (hereinafter referred to as 'manufacturer');
(ii) any person who provides his/her name, trade name, trademark or other indication (hereinafter referred to as 'representation of name, etc'.) on the product as the manufacturer of such product, or any person who provides the representation of name, etc. on the product which misleads the others into believing that he/she is the manufacturer;
(iii) apart from any person mentioned in the preceding item, any person who provides any representation of name, etc. on the product which, in light of the manner concerning the manufacturing, processing, importation or sales of the product, and other circumstances, holds himself/herself out as its substantial manufacturer.

Article 3 (Product Liability)
The manufacturer, etc. shall be liable for damages arising from the infringement of life, body or property of others which is caused by the defect in the delivered product which was manufactured, processed, imported, or provided with the representation of name, etc. described in item 2 or item 3 of paragraph 3 of the preceding Article, provided, however, that the manufacturer, etc. shall not be liable when the damages occur only with respect to such product.

Article 4 (Exemptions)
In cases where Article 3 applies, the manufacturer, etc. shall not be liable as provided in Article 3 if he/she proves that:
(i) the defect in such product could not have been discovered given the state of scientific or technical knowledge at the time when the manufacturer, etc. delivered the product; or
(ii) in case where the product is used as a component or raw material of another product, the defect occurred primarily because of the compliance with the instructions concerning the design given by the manufacturer of such another product, and that the manufacturer, etc. is not negligent with respect to the occurrence of such defect.

Article 5 (Limitation of Period)
(1) The right to seek damages provided in Article 3 shall be extinguished by prescription if the victim or his/her legal representative does not exercise such right within 3 years from the time when he/she becomes aware of the damages and the party liable for the damages. The same shall apply to the case where 10 years have elapsed from the time when the manufacturer, etc. delivered the product.
(2) The period referred to in the second sentence of the preceding paragraph shall be calculated from the time of the occurrence of the damages where such damages are caused by substances which become harmful to human health when they accumulate in the body, or where the symptoms which represent such damages appear after a certain latent period.

Article 6 (Application of Civil Code)
Other than as provided in this Act, the liability of the manufacturer, etc. for damages caused by a defect in a product shall be subject to the provisions of the Civil Code (Act No. 89 of 1896).

167. The main amendment of general tort principles in the Product Liability Act is to shift from fault liability to strict liability. According to Article 3 of the Act, 'The manufacturer, etc. shall be liable for damages arising from the infringement of life, body or property of others which is caused by the defect in the delivered product ... ' Therefore, strict liability shall be imposed on any manufacturer who delivered the defective product, and a victim only needs to prove the existence of 'defect' of the product, not the 'fault' on the side of manufacturer.

168. The victim is still required to prove causation between the defect and the loss, which is sometimes difficult for plaintiff in case the defective parts had already been disappeared. However, case law has attempted to reduce the burden of proving causal relationship between the defect and the loss by applying the method of 'presumption of fact', which allows for plaintiff to submit a fact based on indirect evidence. For detail, see Part V below. There is one case where the victim who ordered orange juice at the first-food restaurant, claimed for compensation of injury at throat under the Product Liability Act, and the court determined, from presuming several indirect evidences, that the juice was the cause of plaintiff's injury by indicating that it cannot be denied the possibility that certain foreign substance was added in the juice in process of manufacturing.[99]

169. The Product Liability Act imposes strict liability on manufacturers, but it also provides provision to exempt liability for them. According to Article 4 of the Act, there are two cases. One is in case that 'the defect in such product could not have been discovered given the state of scientific or technical knowledge at the time when the manufacturer, etc. delivered the product', and another is 'in case where the product is used as a component or raw material of another product, the defect occurred primarily because of the compliance with the instructions concerning the design given by the manufacturer of such another product, and that the manufacturer, etc. is not negligent with respect to the occurrence of such defect'.

170. According to Article 5(1) of the Act, the period to exercise right to claim compensation for damages under this Act is limited to three years, which is consistent with the period in Article 724 of the Civil Code. However, the absolute time period, which was twenty years in the Code, has been reduced to ten years in the Act. For detail, see Part IV, Chapter 1 below.

171. There is also special provision to postpone the starting point (the commencement date) for initiating the absolute time period (ten years) under Article 5(2) of the Act, in case 'where such damages are caused by substances which

99. Nagoya DCJ 30 Jun. 1999 Hanji 1682-106.

become harmful to human health when they accumulate in the body, or where the symptoms which represent such damages appear after a certain latent period'.

172. According to Article 6 of the Act, 'Other than as provided in this Act, the liability of the manufacturer, etc. for damages caused by a defect in a product shall be subject to the provisions of the Civil Code.' Therefore, the provision of 'comparative negligence' in Article 722(2) of the Code or case law applied this provision *mutatis mutandis* shall be applied in the product liability litigations.[100] For detail, see Part VI, Chapter 2, §7 below, see also Part VI, Chapter 3, §4 below.

173. Problem of Product Liability Act is a narrowness of its scope. According to Article 2(1), the defective 'product' which shall be covered under this Act is only 'movable which is manufactured or processed'. Therefore, in case there is a defect in real property, intangible property, energy or service, it is out of the scope of the Product Liability Act. However, there is another special act, Housing Quality Assurance Act enacted in 1999, for dealing with defects on houses.

100. See, e.g., Fukuoka HCJ 15 Dec. 2011 Hanji 2164-61.

Chapter 3. Liability for Service

174. Service is out of the scope of the Product Liability Act. The Act defines the term 'product' as 'movable which is manufactured or processed' (Article 2(1) of the Act) and, the term 'manufacturer' as 'any person who manufactured, processed, or imported the product in the course of trade' (Article 2(3) of the Act). Therefore, there is no room to apply this Act for person who provides service to impose strict liability, even though such service involves certain defect and caused loss to others.

175. Not in the form of strict liability, but internet service provider may be liable for infringement of copyright or injury to reputation (defamation) caused in the internet environment. There are few cases related to the copyright infringement,[101] but there are many cases considering the liability of internet service provider related to defamation. There are cases held that such provider is liable to take appropriate measure to avoid defamation for victim caused by the third party in electronic bulletin board (BBS), and imposed tort liability for providers who failed to do so to compensate damages for victims.[102] However, there is one case held that tort liability for internet service provider should be applied only in the limiting cases, where the aspect of the infringement is malicious or the extent of the damage is enormous.[103] The special act enacted in 2001, called the Provider Liability Limitation Act, restricts on the tort liability for damages of such providers.

101. See, e.g., Tokyo HCJ 3 Mar. 2005 Hanji 1893-126.
102. See, e.g., Tokyo DCJ 26 June 2002 Hanji 1810-78; Tokyo DCJ 25 Jun. 2003 Hanji 1869-54; Tokyo DCJ 17 Jul. 2003 Hanji 1869-46; Tokyo HCJ 17 Jun. 2009 Hanji 2065-50. Cf. Nagoya DCJ 21 Jan. 2005 Hanji 1893-75 (negative).
103. Tokyo DCJ 24 Sep. 1999 Hanji 1707-139.

Chapter 4. Environmental Liability

176. There are several special statutes imposing strict liability in the area of environmental law. The oldest statute is the Mining Act enacted in 1939. Then, as already explained, in 1960s, environmental pollution problem became serious in the Japanese society and there were many related lawsuits in this era. As a result, these lawsuits led to the enactment of the Air Pollution Control Act in 1968, the Water Pollution Control Act in 1971 and the Act on Liability for Oil Pollution Damage in 1975, which are characterized as strict liability legislation. However, each act also prepares a proviso to exempt or reduce liability in case of natural disaster, any other force majeure or so, as below.

177. Article 109(1) (Obligation for Compensation) of the Mining Act states that:

> If others are damaged by excavation of land to mine minerals, discharge of mine water or waste water, heaps of waste rock or slag, or discharge of metallurgical smoke, such damage shall be compensated by the holder of mining right in the mining area concerned at the time of occurrence of damage (or the holder of mining lease right, if a mining lease right is created in the mining area concerned). If the right of mining has already become extinct at the time of occurrence of damage, such damage shall be compensated by the holder of mining right in the mining area concerned at the time of extinction of the mining right (or the holder of mining lease right, if a mining lease right was created in the mining area concerned at the time of extinction of the mining right).

Article 113 (Consideration for Compensation) states that:

> If there is any cause attributable to an aggrieved party concerning occurrence of damage, the court may take such cause into consideration to specify the responsibility and scope of compensation for damage. The same shall apply to the case where natural disasters and other force majeure occur.

178. Article 25(1) of the Air Pollution Control Act states that:

> Where any person suffers fatal or bodily harm from the emission into the atmosphere (including dispersal; hereinafter the same shall apply in this Chapter) of any substance that is harmful to human health (meaning Soot and Smoke, specified substances, or Particulates, and excluding any substance specified by Cabinet Order as posing a risk of damage only to the living environment; hereinafter the same shall apply in this Chapter) associated with business activities at a factory or workplace, the business operator connected with said emissions shall be liable to compensate for any resulting damages.

Article 25-3 (Considerations Regarding Compensation) of the Act states that:

> When a natural disaster or other force majeure is also involved in the occurrence of the damages specified in Article 25, paragraph (1), the court may take

those factors into consideration to determine responsibility and the amount of compensation for damages.

179. Article 19(1) of the Water Pollution Control Act states that:

> In cases where human life or health is damaged by the harmful substances in the polluted water or wastewater discharged (including underground percolation; the same hereinafter in this Chapter) from factories or other establishments as a result of industrial activities the enterpriser is liable for compensating the damage caused thereby.

Article 20-2 (Consideration for Compensation) states that:

> When a natural disaster or any other force majeure is concurrently attributable to the occurrence of the damage provided for in Article 19 Paragraph 1, the Court may take such circumstances into consideration in determining the extent of liability and the sum of compensation.

180. Article 3(1) of the 'Act on Liability for Oil Pollution Damage' also provides similar provisions of strict liability for the business operator. It is stated that:

> When Tanker Oil Pollution Damage occurred, the Tanker Owner of the Tanker in which the Oil pertaining to the said Tanker Oil Pollution Damage was loaded shall be responsible for compensation for the damage, provided, however, that this shall not apply if the said Tanker Oil Pollution Damage falls under any of the following items: (i) Damage was caused by war, civil war or insurrection. (ii) Damage was caused by an abnormal natural disaster. (iii) Damage was solely caused knowingly by the person other than the said Tanker owner or his/her employees. (iv) Damage was solely caused by a defect in the management of the aids to navigation or the signal facilities for traffic control by the state or a public entity.

181. Article 3 of the 'Act on Compensation for Nuclear Damage' enacted in 1961 also imposes strict liability on the nuclear operator for nuclear damages resulting from the operation of nuclear reactor. However, there is a proviso to exempt liability for such nuclear operator in case the damages occurred by abnormally huge natural disasters or social insurrection.

Chapter 5. Others

§1. Strict Liability under the Civil Code

182. As already explained in Part II, the Civil Code imposes strict liability on employer for damages caused to third party by his employees under Article 715 (Liability of Employers), on possessor or owner of any structure on land caused damages to others under Article 717 (Liability of Possessor and Owner of Structure on Land), and on possessor or manager of animals which inflicted on others under Article 718 (Liability of Possessor of Animal). However, there is a proviso in each provision to exempt strict liability for party above, except for the owner of structure of land under Article 717. Therefore, to be precise, the nature of liability in such provisions including such proviso is considered as 'intermediate liability' between fault liability and strict liability.

§2. Other Provisions of Strict Liability

183. According to the 'Act on Prohibition of Private Monopolization and Maintenance of Fair Trade' enacted in 1947, Article 25(1) states that:

> A enterprise that has committed an act in violation of the provisions of Articles 3, 6 or 19 (for enterprises that have committed acts in violation of the provisions of Article 6, limited to enterprises that have effected unreasonable restraint of trade or employed unfair trade practices in the international agreement or contract concerned) and any trade association that has committed an act in violation of the provisions of Article 8 is liable for damages suffered by another party.

Then, Article 25(2) states that 'No enterprise or trade association may be exempted from the liability provided in the preceding paragraph by proving the non-existence of intention or negligence on its part.'

Article 3 prohibits for enterprise to effect private monopolization or unreasonable restraint of trade. Article 6 prohibits for enterprise to enter into an international agreement or an international contract which contains such matters as fall under unreasonable restraint of trade or unfair trade practices. Article 19 prohibits for enterprise to employ unfair trade practices. Article 8 prohibits for trade association to engage in any act, such as substantially restraining competition in any particular field of trade, entering into an international agreement or an international contract as provided in Article 6, limiting the present or future number of enterprises in any particular field of business, unjustly restricting the functions or activities of the constituent enterprises, or inducing enterprises to employ such act as falls under unfair trade practices.

Strict liability shall be imposed on any enterprise or trade association which was against the provisions above.

184. There are some provisions of strict liability in the Financial Instruments and Exchange Act enacted in 1948, such as Article 16 (Liability for Damages for Violating Article 15),[104] Article 18 (Liability for Damages of Person Who Submits Securities Registration Statement Containing Fake Statement, etc.), and Article 21-2 (Liability for Damages of Person Who Submits Document Containing Fake Statement, etc.).

104. Article 15 is the provision for 'Prohibition of Transaction of Securities for Which Notification has Not Yet Come into Effect, and Delivery of Prospectus'.

Part IV. Defences and Exception Clauses

Chapter 1. Limitation of Action

185. The general provisions of 'prescription' covering both 'acquisitive prescription' and 'extinctive prescription' are provided from Articles 144–161 in the Part I (General Part) of the Civil Code, and the specific provisions for 'extinctive prescription' are provided from Articles 166–174-2 in the Part I of the Code as well. However, there is a special provision for 'extinctive prescription' or 'statute of limitation' to restrict the period of right to demand compensation for damages by tort in the Part III of the Code. According to Article 724 of the Code:

> The right to demand compensation for damages in tort shall be extinguished by the operation of prescription if it is not exercised by the victim or his/her legal representative within three years from the time when he/she comes to know of the damages and the identity of the perpetrator. The same shall apply when twenty years have elapsed from the time of the tortious act.

It is necessary to refer to both related provisions in Part I and Article 724 in Part III of the Code to understand this system.

186. The period to exercise right to claim compensation for damages in tort is limited to three years, according to the first sentence of Article 724. This is a very short extinctive period in comparison with the period in other law. For example, a claim based on contract 'shall be extinguished if not exercised for ten years' under Article 167(1) of the Civil Code.

187. Then, Article 144 of the Code states that 'The prescription shall take effect retroactively as of the commencement day.' Therefore, it is important to set the commencement day to make the prescription effect, and Article 724 provides evaluation criteria for claim in tort law specifically, that is, from the time when the victim or his/her legal representative 'comes to know of the damages and the identity of the perpetrator'. According to case law, the term 'know of the damages' means that the victim recognized in reality the occurrence of damage caused by tortfeasor,[105] and, the term 'know the identity of the perpetrator' means that the victim recognized the tortfeasor to the extent that the claims can be fulfilled effectively.[106] It should be

105. SCJ 29 Jan. 2002 Minshu 56-1-218.
106. SCJ 16 Nov. 1973 Minshu 27-10-1374.

noted that, in case the employer is liable to his employee's tort liability under Article 715, or, in case the joint tortfeasors are liable to victim under Article 719, the term 'perpetrator' or 'tortfeasor' in Article 724 is not a proper term, so it should be read as the 'person who is obliged to compensate'.

188. There is another period to exercise right to claim compensation for damages in the second sentence of Article 724, that is, 'when twenty years have elapsed from the time of the tortious act'. Case law and majority of academic consider this twenty years period as an absolute time period stated by the policy.[107] The differences between the 'three years period' and the 'twenty years period' are follows: First, the 'interruption of prescription' under Article 147 is only applicable in case of 'three year period'. In case any prescription is interrupted by: (i) any claim, (ii) any attachment, provisional seizure, or provisional disposition, or (iii) any acknowledgment under this provision, it takes effect to reset the commencement date 'at the time the applicable grounds for suspension cease to exist' under Article 157(1), or 'at the time of the final and binding judgment' in case of judicial claim under Article 157(2). Second, as a requirement to take effect the prescription, the related party has to invoke it at the court under Article 145, but this is only required in case of 'three year period'. Therefore, it could be concluded that the right to demand compensation for damages in tort shall be extinguished once the twenty years elapsed from the time of the tortious act, without considering the interruption or invocation of prescription. However, the 'suspension of prescription' under Articles 160 and 161 are applicable to both 'three years period' and the 'twenty years period'.

189. As mentioned above, the extinctive period in tort law is three years and it is considered as very short period, even though the starting point for initiating this period sets, in fact, from the time when the victim or his/her legal representative 'comes to know of the damages and the identity of the perpetrator'. Case law has attempted to postpone this starting point (the commencement date) in various situations, because damage caused by tort is not necessarily to be expressed immediately at the moment the tortious act has been done.

190. For example, there is a case that after-effect has been expressed for a while after the tortious act, and the Supreme Court determined the starting point for this loss from the date when the after-effect becomes apparent.[108]

191. Another example is the case that tort has been carried out continuously, and as a result, several damages may also occur separately and continuously. In such a case, the Supreme Tribunal stated that, as long as the damage caused to each another by the continuing tort, the extinctive prescription for each individual damage shall proceed to damage for each.[109]

107. SCJ 21 Dec. 1989 Minshu 43-12-2209.
108. SCJ 18 Jul. 1967 Minshu 21-6-1559.
109. STJ (Civil Affairs Union) 14 Dec. 1940 Minshu 19-2325.

192. The more recent cases deal with the 'damage accumulation type' or 'damage progressive type'. This is the case where the latent damage was not expressed immediately but expressed on after a long period of time, or the damage is of progressive and such damage has been expanded the years. Such damages are typically found in 'pneumoconiosis (lung disease caused by dust inhalation) litigations'. There is a related statutory provision in Article 115(2) of the Mining Act enacted in 1950. This is the provision of extinctive prescription, which states that 'As for damage in progress, the period prescribed in the preceding paragraph shall commence from the day when the progress thereof ceases.' In the recent pneumoconiosis litigations, the Supreme Court has attempted to postpone the starting point for initiating the extinctive period of Article 724 of the Civil Code. In 1994, the Court sets the starting point at the moment when the final administrative decision has been received based on the classification for supervision of pneumoconiosis under the Pneumoconiosis Act.[110] In 2004, the Supreme Court made the judgment related to this issue, and it held that the starting point for initiating the extinctive period for 'twenty years period' shall be set at the moment of the victim's death.[111]

110. SCJ 22 Feb. 1994 Minshu 48-2-441.
111. SCJ 27 Oct. 2004 Minshu 58-4-1032.

Chapter 2. Grounds of Justification

193. To establish tort liability it is required that a tortious act has unlawfulness. In other words, in case such an act could be justified on some grounds, there is no unlawfulness and, in effect, tort liability would not be established. The Civil Code only has a provision of 'self-defense' and 'aversion of present danger' in Article 720, but, as a matter of course, there are other grounds of justification admitted by case law and academic.

§1. Consent

194. The 'consent by victim' is considered as one of the grounds of justification for tortfeasor's act, even though there is no provision in the Civil Code, but such a justification should be properly limited from the viewpoint of 'public policy' (Article 90 of the Civil Code). Therefore, the consent by victim to the infringement to his life or body, for example, in case of 'euthanasia', should not be allowed from this reason.

§2. Necessity

195. Article 720(2) in the Civil Code states that 'The provisions of the preceding paragraph[112] shall apply mutatis mutandis to cases where a Thing belonging to others is damaged to avoid imminent danger arising from that Thing.' It should be noted that the justification of acts under this provision is limited to 'a Thing belonging to others'. However, Article 37 of the Penal Code has a similar provision of 'Averting present Danger', but the scope of the justification is wider than that of the Civil Code. It states that:

> An act unavoidably performed to avert a present danger to the life, body, liberty or property of oneself or any other person is not punishable only when the harm produced by such act does not exceed the harm to be averted; provided, however, that an act causing excessive harm may lead to the punishment being reduced or may exculpate the offender in light of the circumstances.

Therefore, it shall be applied in case 'to avert a present danger to the life, body, liberty or property of oneself or any other person' in criminal case.

---

112. Article 720(1) of the Civil Code provides that 'A person who, in response to the tortious act of another, unavoidably commits a harmful act to protect himself/herself, the rights of a third party, or any legally protected interest, shall not be liable for damages; provided, however, that the victim shall not be precluded from claiming damages against the person who committed the tortious act'.

§3. Self-Help and Self-Defence

196. In principle, 'self-help' is prohibited because it is expected for citizens to realize their rights by legal proceedings. Therefore, self-help is also not allowed in tort law. However, according to the Supreme Court in 1965,[113] at the obiter dictum, when there is an infringement to the right, self-help may be permitted in exceptional circumstances within a range that does not exceed the extent necessary, namely, in case that there are special circumstances where unavoidable emergency exists, such as it is found to be impossible or extremely difficult to maintain the status quo if only relying on legal proceedings.

197. There is a provision of 'self-defense' in Article 720(1) of the Civil Code and it states that:

> A person who, in response to the tortious act of another, unavoidably commits a harmful act to protect himself/herself, the rights of a third party, or any legally protected interest, shall not be liable for damages; provided, however, that the victim shall not be precluded from claiming damages against the person who committed the tortious act.

198. The object of this provision is as same as the similar provision of 'self-defense' in Article 36(1) of the Penal Code, which states that 'An act unavoidably performed to protect the rights of oneself or any other person against imminent and unlawful infringement is not punishable'. However, in case of 'excessive self-defense', tort liability may be established with considering the 'contributory fault' (Article 722(2)) of the victim who exercised the excessive self-defence. The object of this provision is also consistent with Article 36(2) of the Penal Code, which states that 'An act exceeding the limits of self-defense may lead to the punishment being reduced or may exculpate the offender in light of the circumstances.'

§4. Others

199. As well as the Penal Code states that 'An act performed in accordance with laws and regulations or in the pursuit of lawful business is not punishable' in Article 35, the Civil law also allows 'lawful business' as a justifiable acts. There are several acts included in this category and no tort liability would be established in such situations. Legitimate act of surgery by doctor, or legitimate act by police is the typical examples, but the following cases may be also regarded as a justifiable act.

200. First, 'act to bring in lawsuit' is considered as a justifiable act, as long as it is not deviant from the purpose of court system. There is a Supreme Court case that lawsuit against defendant by plaintiff is regarded as an unlawful act when there was

113. SCJ 7 Dec. 1965 Minshu 19-9-2101 (obiter dictum).

no cause of action and the plaintiff knew or should have known it, but he dared to bring in lawsuit.[114]

201. Second, 'act of game' is also considered as a justifiable act. There is a case that the father is not liable under Article 714 of the Civil Code for his 7 years old daughter's act breaking her friend's bone during playing tag by this reason.[115] Similarly, 'act of sport' among players shall be justified not only because of the 'consent [to join sport] by victims' as mentioned above, but also because of the lawfulness of playing sport. However, this justification shall not be applied to the third party who is not the player, but suffered a loss thereby.[116]

202. Under the Labor Union Act enacted in 1949, 'a Strike or other acts of dispute' is regarded as a justifiable act. According to Article 8 of the Act, 'An employer may not make a claim for damages against a labour union or a union member for damages received through a strike or other acts of dispute which are justifiable acts'.

203. Further, 'disciplinary action' to the child by person who exercises parental authority (Article 822(1) of the Civil Code) or by teachers (Article 11 of the School Education Act) are considered as justifiable act to the extent necessary.

114. SCJ 26 Jan. 1988 Minshu 42-1-1.
115. SCJ 27 Feb. 1962 Minshu 16-2-407.
116. SCJ 10 Mar. 1995 Hanji 1526-99.

Chapter 3. Contributory Fault

204. In the Civil Code of Japan, there is an explicit provision of 'comparative negligence' in tort law (Article 722(2)), not the 'contributory fault or negligence' which used to see in the common-law countries. These two rules are common in respect of considering victim's negligence, but there are differences in the legal effect. That is, in case the 'contributory negligence' is applied, the tortfeasor becomes not liable in such a way that the plaintiff's claim is prohibited, regardless of the degree of victim's negligence. However, in case the 'comparative negligence' is applied, the tortfeasor is still liable, but the court shall determine – more specifically 'reduce' – the 'amount of compensation' by considering the degree of victim's negligence. The 'comparative negligence' serves to mitigate the damages, therefore, it will be explained later at §7, Chapter 2 of Part VI.

Chapter 4. Exemption Clauses

205. In general, according to the principle of 'freedom of contract', parties may agree on exemption clauses in their contract, and, in addition, provisions related to contract law are default clauses, therefore, exemption clauses for contract liability are valid. However, provisions related to tort law under the Civil Code or other related statutes are mandatory clauses, therefore, exemption clauses for tort liability are void.

206. What if contractual parties attempt to include some exemption clauses for tort liability in their contract? Even in such a case, the law tends to restrict the validity of such clauses. There are related explicit provisions in the Consumer Contract Act enacted in 2001. Under Article 8(1) of the Act, 'Clauses which totally exempt a Business Operator from liability for damages to a Consumer which arise from a tort pursuant to the provisions of the Civil Code committed during the Business Operator's performance of a Consumer Contract' (Clause III), and, 'Clauses which partially exempt a Business Operator from liability for damages to a Consumer arising from a tort (limited to cases in which the same arises due to an intentional act or gross negligence on the part of the Business Operator, the Business Operator's representative or employee) pursuant to the provisions of the Civil Code committed during the Business Operator's performance of a Consumer Contract' (Clause IV) are void.

Part V. Causation

§1. Concept of Causation

207. Case law has been used the term 'causation' in two different situations, therefore there are two different functions in causation. One is as a requirement to establish general tort liability on Article 709 of the Civil Code, so that it is required to have the causal relationship between the act of tortfeasor and the loss of victim. The other is as a method of assessing damages. The latter issue will be discussed at §3, Chapter 3 of Part VI.

208. The causal relationship between the act and the loss is required to establish tort liability so that it has to be proved in court that such loss would have occurred but for the act of the tortfeasor. In principle, the plaintiff (victim) owes the burden of proof of such causation between the act and the loss. It is not so difficult to prove such causation in case of typical traffic accidents, but, for example, in case of environmental pollution litigations or malpractice litigations the plaintiff may face difficulty to prove it. Case law has kept a stance to relax this requirement, and it is already confirmed by the Supreme Court that the 'causation' as a legal term is not equal with the level expected in natural science, but the necessary and enough level to satisfy this requirement is a 'high probability' of causation to the extent that reasonable person is not suspected.[117]

209. Proof of causation is a heavy burden for the plaintiff. Thus, case law has attempted several ways to reduce the burden of proving causal relationship between tortious act and loss. One of the typical methods is the 'prima facie presumption', which has been used in the trial practice conventionally, and it would evaluate the estimated fact proved by the plaintiff as the fact, unless the defendant rebuts this estimation.[118] Another method is the 'presumption of fact', which allows for plaintiff to submit a fact based on indirect evidence, and then court will infer another fact from there, unless the defendant rebuts this indirect evidence. For example, from the indirect evidence of 'drunken driving', the fact of 'improper driving' will be presumed. There is one case where the court stated that there was a defect in the freezer manufactured by the defendant, and determined that the freezer was the cause of a

117. SCJ 24 Oct. 1975 Minshu 29-9-1417.
118. *Ibid.*

fire in the shop of the plaintiff from presuming several indirect evidences.[119] Whatever the case may be, these methods have served to shift the burden of proof from plaintiff to defendant.

210. In most cases of malpractice litigation, tortious acts by doctor is 'forbearance', therefore, it is more difficult to prove causal relationship between 'not taking appropriate medical care' and 'the loss of victims' such as early death. Courts have admitted such loss as an infringement of 'protected interest of patient's long life' and stated that, in case that the patient would have had a long life if the doctor had taken the appropriate treatment, it is enough to prove the 'high probability' or 'considerable possibility' of causation between the 'inappropriate medical care' and the 'early death'.[120] There is also a case, in case the patient would not have remained serious after-effects if the doctor had taken the appropriate treatment, to accept the proof of 'considerable possibility' of causation between the 'inappropriate medical care' and the 'serious aftereffects'.[121]

§2. Joint Tort Liability

211. In this Part V, 'joint tort liability' stated in Article 719 of the Civil Code will be also discussed, because this Article as a special provision of tort law modifies the requirement of 'causation' under Article 709 in case there are several tortfeasors.

212. According to Article 719(1), it states that:

> If more than one person has inflicted damages on others by their joint tortious acts, each of them shall be jointly and severally liable to compensate for those damages. The same shall apply if it cannot be ascertained which of the joint tortfeasors inflicted the damages.

Then, according to Article 719(2), it states that 'The provisions of the preceding paragraph shall apply to any person who incited or was an accessory to the perpetrator, by deeming him/her to be one of the joint tortfeasors.'

213. There are several situations where Article 719 shall be applied. First, there is an 'Integrated tortious acts' type (Type I), which is derived from the first sentence of Article 719(1), where there are more than one tortious acts, but it is considered as a one tortious act. For example, when C was injured by adding assault in conspiracy of A and B, in such a case, A and B are jointly liable to C under Article 719(1).

119. Tokyo DCJ 31 Oct. 1999 Hanji 1687-39.
120. See, e.g., SCJ 25 Feb. 1999 Minshu 53-2-235; SCJ 22 Sep. 2000 Minshu 54-7-2574.
121. See, SCJ 11 Nov. 2003 Minshu 57-10-1466.

214. Second, there is a 'Tortfeasors unknown' type (Type II), which is derived from the second sentence of Article 719(1), where there is a tortious act by more than one tortfeasors, but it is not clear who causes the damage to victim. For example, when C was seriously injured by A and B who opened fire by mistaking C for a bear, but only one bullet hit C and it is unknown whether the bullet was fired from A or B, A and B are jointly liable to C under Article 719(1).

215. Third, there is 'Aid and Abet' type (Type III), which is derived from Article 719(2), where, in the example of 'Type I' above, D aided and abetted A and B to add assault against C, D is also liable with A and B jointly to C.

216. Finally, there is a case where Article 719 shall be applied *mutatis mutandis*, and it may be called 'Integrated damages' type (Type IV). In such a case, there are more than one tortious acts separately, but it is considered that these acts caused the integrated damages to the victim. For example, where C is met with a traffic accident resulting from driver A's negligence, then, there is a medical errors in the hospital resulting from doctor B's negligence, and eventually C died, or where A factory and B factory shed effluent to the same river separately, and those acts caused a health hazard to residents of the village C. In such cases, even both A's act and B's act could be considered separately, A and B are jointly liable to C because it seems that both acts causes integrated damages to C.

217. The 'causation' between the tortfeasor's act and the victim's loss, as a requirement to establish general tort liability, would not be properly applied in cases of Type I to IV mentioned above. In any of the cases, it is almost impossible to prove the causal relationship between the tortious acts by more than one tortfeasors (A, B, D) and the loss caused by C. In either case, regardless of the requirements of causation, each of tortfeasors 'shall be jointly and severally liable to compensate for those damages'. Therefore, the scope of the joint tortfeasors is to emerge as a more important issue in these situations. So, on behalf of the requirement of causation, case law applies the requirement of 'related cooperativity' (*Kanren-Kyodosei*) to establish joint liability under Article 719, as will be discussed below. However, other requirements to establish general tort liability, such as fault, unlawfulness, and capacity, shall be required even in case of joint liability covered by Article 719.

218. To establish joint tort liability, it is necessary that each tortfeasor's act has 'related cooperativity', and, according to case law and academic, there are two criteria of 'related cooperativity', that is, 'subjective' one and 'objective' one. As for the former criteria, the subjective related cooperativity means that there is a strong subjective 'joint intention' among the related tortfeasors. Therefore, in case of Type I where there was 'conspiracy' between A and B, or Type III where there was 'aid and abet' of D, it is easy to determine the subjective joint intention among the parties, therefore, those parties are jointly liable to C because of satisfying the requirement of subjective related cooperativity, without considering the causation between the acts and the loss. There is one Supreme Court case,[122] which stated that, even though there was no conspiracy or no subjective joint intention among the parties, subjective related cooperativity shall be recognized in case the damages resulting from one or more tortfeasors was huge and serious.

219. However, case law has adopted and developed the latter criteria, that is, the objective related cooperativity, especially in environmental pollution litigations. It means that, according to the Supreme Court case in 1968,[123] without considering the subjective joint intention among tortfeasors, if each of those acts has a 'related cooperativity' when viewed objectively, as long as each act has been satisfied the general tort requirements separately, each of them shall be liable to compensate the damages, to the extent of reasonable causation between each act and the loss. Then, the following lower level court cases have developed these criteria in more detail. The trial court case in 1972[124] has subdivided the objective related cooperativity into 'weak' one and 'strong' one, and in case it is determined that one of the tortfeasor has a 'strong' related cooperativity, such person shall be liable to compensate the damages, without considering the causation between the total result of acts and the loss. Then, the trial court case in 1991 has attempted to clarify the differences of legal effect between the 'weak' and 'strong' criteria above.[125] According to this court, all of the tortfeasors are jointly liable to the loss whether or not he has either of the related cooperativity, but in case of weak one, such party may be exempt or reduce from the liability, but in case of strong one, such party has no room for exemption or reduction of liability.

220. In case of 'Integrated damages' type (Type IV), it is difficult to apply both 'subjective' and 'objective' related cooperativity, because more than one tortious acts exists separately, but only the damages caused to the victim is considered to integrate by such separate tortious acts. The Supreme Court case in 2001,[126] in case where the victim had met with a traffic accident, then, there was a medical error in the hospital, and eventually he died, applied the different criteria, that is, the concept of 'inseparable result', and stated that both tortfeasors, the driver and the doctor, were jointly liable on the ground that each of the acts caused the death of victims which is considered as an inseparable result.

122. SCJ 22 Jan. 1987 Minshu 41-1-17.
123. SCJ 23 Apr. 1968 Minshu 22-4-964.
124. Tsu DCJ (Yokkaichi Division) 24 Jul. 1972 Hanji 672-30.
125. Osaka DCJ 29 Mar. 1991 Hanji 1383-22.
126. SCJ 13 Mar. 2001 Minshu 55-2-328.

Part VI. Remedies

Chapter 1. General Principles

221. In principle, the amount of damages shall be determined with reference to monetary value. Article 722(1) of the Civil Code states that 'The provisions of Article 417 shall apply mutatis mutandis to compensation for damages in tort', and then, Article 417 of the Civil Code states that 'Unless other intention is manifested, the amount of the damages shall be determined with reference to monetary value'.

222. As an exception to the above, the court may order the injuring party to take restoration (restitutional) measures for the victim. Article 723 (Recovery in Defamation) of the Civil Code states that 'The court may, at the request of the victim, order a person who defamed others, to effect appropriate measures to restore the reputation of the victim in lieu of, or in addition to, damages.' In addition, Article 14 (Measures to restore business reputation) of the Unfair Competition Prevention Act enacted in 1993 states that 'At the request of a person whose business reputation has been injured, the court may order the person who has intentionally or negligently engaged in unfair competition and thereby injured the business reputation of that person to take the necessary measures for restoring the business reputation of that person, in lieu of or in addition to compensation for damages.' The 'appropriate measures' or 'necessary measures' indicated in above provisions means 'public announcement of apology', and it is usually taken by posting such announcement in the newspaper.

223. Another exception is the 'injunctive relief'. There is no clear provision in the Civil Code, but it is frequently claimed in environmental pollution cases or cases of infringement of reputation and privacy. For detail, see Chapter 7, §2 below.

224. The Civil Code provides no provision clearly prescribing the definitions and categories of damage and the nature of the respective categories of damage. Also, there is no special statutory provision in tort law, expressly defining the scope of the damages to be compensated. Therefore, it is important to understand the jurisprudence developed by case law.

Chapter 2. Kinds of Damages

§1. Individual and Collective Damage

225. In principle, Japanese tort law only allows individual damage, but recently a new legislation opens the way to authorize the class action lawsuits. It is the 'Act on Special Measure for Civil Procedure in Collective Restoration of the Consumer Financial Damage', which was promulgated in 11 December 2013 and the effective date of this Act shall be within three years from that day.

226. The Consumer Contract Act (2001) has been already authorized the 'Qualified Consumer Organizations' to demand injunctive relief for 'many and unspecified consumers' against a business operator or related parties to unlawful acts which was prohibited under Articles 4, 8, 9 and 10 of the Act, when this Act was amended in 2007 (See Articles 12–47 of the Act). The new Act just promulgated in 2013 allows the same 'organizations' to demand compensation of collective damage for 'a considerable number of consumer' against a business operator. The claims under this new Act is limited to that could be claimed under the Consumer Contract Act, on the grounds of claims for performance of contract, for compensation of damages resulting from breach of contract, breach of warranty or tort, and for unjust enrichment (Article 3(1) of the Act). However, in case such organization demands compensation under this Act, so-called extended damage, lost profits, damages for personal injury or death, and *solatium* shall be excluded from the scope of collective damage (Article 3(2) of the Act). To this extent, collective damage would be allowed in near future by this Act.

§2. Direct and Indirect Damage

I. The Subject of Claimants

227. Before we start to discuss the concept of direct and indirect damages, it is necessary to make clear the subject of claimants who are able to compensate damages under tort law. In this respect, not only the 'natural person' and the 'juridical person' but also the 'unborn child' can be the claimant.

228. An unborn child is entitled to claim compensation for damages. According to Article 3(1) of the Civil Code, 'The enjoyment of private rights shall commence at birth.' Therefore, in principle, unborn child has no capacity to hold private rights, but the Civil Code provides two exceptions for unborn child to allow legal capacity. One is the right relating to inheritance (Article 886) and the other is the right to demand compensation for damages in tort (Article 721). Article 721 states that 'An unborn child shall be deemed to have been already born with respect to the right to demand compensation for damages.' However, according to case law and majority of academic, such right for unborn child shall become effective *ex post facto* upon fulfilment of the condition precedent, that is, the birth.[127]

229. A judicial person can naturally claim compensation for the pecuniary loss, but it has been discussed whether the judicial person can also claim for the non-pecuniary loss, because such loss mostly means 'mental suffering' which is difficult to assume for judicial person. However, the Supreme Court allows the claim for non-pecuniary loss by the judicial person who received defamation, on the grounds that non-pecuniary loss is not limited to mental suffering, but covers any type of intangible losses.[128]

II. The Scope of Claimants

230. On the premise of the 'subject of claimants', then, it becomes possible to consider which subject may include in the 'scope of claimants'. In case any subject above is the direct victim who received the infringement of his rights or legally protected interest by tortfeasor, he may claim for such 'direct damage' as long as there is causal relationship between the tortious act and the loss.

231. In case any subject is a third party (indirect victim) having a relationship with the victim indirectly suffers damage, such damage is considered as 'indirect damage' and this problem can be classified into a case of 'personal injury or death' and in a case of 'corporate losses'.

232. In case of personal death, the next of kin of the victim, such as the father, mother, spouse and children of the victim, respectively has the right to claim *solatium* of his/her own under Article 711 of the Civil Code. For detail, see Chapter 4 below. Meanwhile, the right to demand compensation of damages entitled to the victim (both pecuniary losses and non-pecuniary losses) extinguishes upon his/her death. However, the Japanese case law upholds that such right to demand compensation of damages can be succeeded to by his/her heirs. Therefore, such heirs of the victim can also be the claimant for tort damage. This issue will be explained in Chapter 4 of Part VI.

233. In case of personal injury, the victim is entitled to demand compensation for damage for his/her own, however, his next of kin may also suffer property losses for making payment of expenses on behalf of the victim. Case law has allowed the claim for damage from indirect victims, such as medical expenses and nursing care expenses,[129] travel expenses for nursing,[130] etc., which were paid by the victim's next of kin. In addition, in case the next of kin's loss of his own property occurs,

127. STJ 6 Oct. 1932 Minshu 11-2023 (allowing the claim of non-pecuniary loss for unborn child against the railway company who caused the traffic accident and the death of the child's father therefrom.).
128. SCJ 28 Jan. 1964 Minshu 18-1-136.
129. See, SCJ 29 Jun. 1971 Minshu 25-4-650.
130. See, SCJ 25 Apr. 1974 Minshu 28-3-447.

such as lost profits due to absence from work for nursing the victim who was injured, it is also considered as genuine indirect damage.

234. In case of corporate losses, case law has hesitated to allow genuine indirect damages for company when, for example, representative or employee of the company was died or injured by the traffic accident, and as a result, it caused loss of revenue to the company. There is one case where a company claims compensation for genuine indirect damage, and the court held that a company shall be allowed to exercise its right to demand compensation of its income losses, only in an extremely limited case where the victim and the company are deemed substantially identical in terms of their economical relationship.[131] In principle, it is expected for company to take measures in advance so as to cope with any accident of its members.

§3. Pecuniary and Non-pecuniary Losses

235. Pecuniary losses can be measured by money, and it may include 'actual loss' which means loss or detriment to the existing interest of victim, and, 'lost profits' which means loss of interest which the victim would have earned if the tort did not occur. However, non-pecuniary loss cannot be measured by money because it is constituted by mental suffering of victim or victim's family.

236. If a person suffers any non-pecuniary loss (i.e., mental loss), such person is entitled to claim 'solatium' for such loss under Article 710 (Compensation for Damages Other than Property) of the Civil Code. Also, Article 711 (Compensation for Damages to Next of Kin) of the Civil Code entitles the victim's next of kin to claim *solatium* when the victim dies. For detail of these two Articles, see Chapter 4 below. The monetary awarding of *solatium* is at the sole discretion of the judge. Therefore, plaintiff does not have to owe any burden of proof in claiming such non-pecuniary loss.

237. It is discussed whether a *solatium* has a function as a penalty. This issue will be discussed at §3, Chapter 7 of this Part VI.

§4. Pure Economic Loss

238. Pure economic loss may define as damage not resulting from infringement of rights of others. Harmful rumours following a natural disaster, environmental pollution, a leak of radioactivity, and so on may consider as a typical example of pure economic loss. There is few cases claiming for such loss, but theoretically, general tort provision under Article 709 of the Civil Code seems not to exclude such loss, because, tort liability is intended to establish not only in case of infringement of rights of others but also that of protected interest of others.[132] Therefore, there is

131. See, SCJ 15 Nov. 1968 Minshu 22-12-2614.
132. For detail of protected interest of others', see Part I, Ch. 1, s. 1.

a possibility to cover such pure economic loss resulting from harmful rumour by reason of the infringement of commercial benefits. Also, in assessing damage, as long as there is adequate causation between tortious act and the damages occurred, such damages including pure economic loss would be within the scope of damages.[133]

§5. Actual and Future Damage (Lost Profits)

239. As already mentioned above, 'actual loss' means loss or detriment to the existing interest of victim. For example, in case of car accident, losses to the victim's property, that is, breakdown of automobile may be compensated. In such a case, the losses to be compensated are the repair costs, but, in an exceptional case, the purchasing costs of the replacement items may also be compensated.[134] Medical and hospital expenses may also be covered as the actual loss caused by the tortious act. In such a case, the amount within the scope objectively deemed reasonable can be compensated.

240. 'Lost profits' means loss of interest which the victim would have earned if the tort did not occur, and the formula for calculation of lost profits becomes critical issue in case where the victim died by tortious act. For detail, see Chapter 4 below.

§6. Other Costs

241. Funeral expenses can also be compensated, as such expenses are borne by the surviving family members as an unavoidable consequence of the tort.[135]

242. Attorney's fees also can be compensated, as there would have been no need for instituting any litigation if the tort did not occur.[136]

243. Expenses, such as costs of caregivers,[137] fee for future nursing care services, or travel expenses for visiting the victim,[138] can also be compensated.

§7. Mitigation of Damages

244. In the Civil Code of Japan, there is an explicit provision of 'comparative negligence' in Article 722(2). It is stated that 'If a victim is negligent, the court may determine the amount of compensation by taking that factor into consideration.'

133. For detail of adequate causation in assessing damage, see Part VI, Ch. 3, s. 3.
134. SCJ 15 Apr. 1974 Minshu 28-3-385.
135. See, STJ 2 Dec. 1924 Minshu 3-522; SCJ 28 Feb. 1969 Minshu 23-2-525.
136. See, SCJ 27 Feb. 1969 Minshu 23-2-441.
137. See, SCJ 29 Jun. 1971 Minshu 25-4-650.
138. See, SCJ 25 Apr. 1974 Minshu 28-3-447.

Therefore, in case the negligence on the side of the victim contributed to the occurrence or aggravation of the damages arising from the tortious act committed by the injuring party, the court may apply this provision and mitigate the injuring party's obligation for compensation of damages by taking into account such negligence at the discretion of the judge. This provision may also be applied in case of 'both-to-blame' case. For example, if the bicycle collision accident occurs due to negligence of both A and B, both have the right to claim damages to the other party, but each of the damages may be mitigated by considering the degrees of each negligence.

245. For the purpose of application of comparative negligence, it would be sufficient if the victim has the 'capacity to pay attention to avoid occurrence of damage'. It should be noted that this capacity is different with the capacity 'to recognize the liability on the side of tortfeasor', which is required to establish tort liability under Article 712 or 713 of the Civil Code. In addition, the criteria for each of the capacity are different. Twelve years old is a benchmark for the capacity to recognize the liability on the side of tortfeasor. On the other hand, around eight years old is a benchmark for the capacity to pay attention to avoid occurrence of damage on the side of victim, according to case law.[139]

246. According to case law, the negligence to be taken account in Article 722(2) is the negligence 'on the side of the victim'. A party 'on the side of the victim' means a party which is deemed inseparably related to the victim in terms of their social status or livelihood. There is a case where a 2 or 3 year-old child suddenly ran into the road and was hit by an automobile; the court upheld that comparative negligence could be applied, finding that the negligence by the child's parents who had liability to supervise the child could be deemed as 'negligence on the side of the victim'.[140] On the contrary, there is a case where the court determined that the victim's nursery teacher cannot be deemed as a 'party which is deemed inseparably related to the victim'.[141]

139. SCJ (FB) 24 Jun. 1964 Minshu 18-5-854.
140. SCJ 26 Nov. 1959 Minshu 13-12-1573.
141. SCJ 27 Jun. 1967 Minshu 21-6-1507.

Chapter 3. Assessment and Compensation of Damages

§1. Objective versus Subjective

247. Under Japanese tort law, the terms 'objective' and 'subjective' are rarely used in the context of assessment and compensation of damages. Most of the pecuniary losses would be assessed objectively; however, the non-pecuniary losses which mean emotional harm would be assessed subjectively by the discretion of judges in awarding the *solatium.*

§2. Concrete versus Abstract

248. The Civil Code has no provision defining the notion of damage, but case law and majority of academic follow the 'difference' theory (*Sagaku-Setsu*), which has been developed under the influence of German law, and which recognizes the notion of 'damage' as the difference between the actual condition where the tort exists ('present interest standing'), and the condition which would have never existed if the tort did not occur ('hypothetical interest standing').

249. For example, in cases where a victim dies or suffers injury, 'money actually incurred as a result of death or injury (actual loss)', 'money which the victim would have earned if he/she was not killed or injured (lost profits)' and 'solatium' constitute damages, which show the difference between the present situation where the tort existed and the hypothetical situation where the tort would not have existed.

250. However, it is also true that there is a criticism against the 'difference' theory, because, according to this theory, it follows that, when a person dies or suffers any injury, the amount of compensation varies with the income of the victim. Therefore, this criticism suggests that 'human lives shall be treated in a non-discriminatory manner', and the fact of death or injury itself should be recognized as damage when a person dies or suffers any injury (*Songai-Jijitu-Setsu*). This suggestion is not adopted by case law and majority of academic, but the significance of this criticism is that it served to promote standardization of the amount of damages to be compensated.

251. In summary, as long as the 'difference' theory is supported, it can be said the notion of damage is recognized abstractly. However, in fact, case law and law practices are based on this theory, but consider this 'difference' in a manner that piling up the each damage separately, such as lost profits, hospital expenses, medical expenses, nursing care expenses, alimony, funeral expenses, attorneys' fees and so on. In this sense, it can be said the notion of damage is recognized concretely or specifically.

§3. Methods of Assessing Damages

252. The tort law does not have any express provision defining the scope of compensation of damages. The Supreme Tribunal upheld the analogical application of the provision of Article 416 of the Civil Code (scope of damages for failure to perform obligations) to the case of identification of the scope of damages in tort.[142] Article 416 states as follows:

> Article 416 (Scope of Damages)
> (1) The purpose of the demand for the damages for failure to perform an obligation shall be to demand the compensation for damages which would ordinarily arise from such failure.
> (2) The obligee may also demand the compensation for damages which arise from any special circumstances if the party did foresee, or should have foreseen, such circumstances.
> Article 416 of the Civil Code provides for the criteria to identify the scope of damages. In principle, the scope is 'damages which would ordinarily arise from the failure' (Article 416(1)); and, in exceptional cases, 'damages which arise from any special circumstances' can be claimed (Article 416(2)).

253. The court interprets the provision of Article 416 of the Civil Code as providing for the compensation of damages where there is adequate causation between the default in performance of obligation and the damage occurred. This is called 'theory of adequate causation'. The court's holding is that the purpose of this provision is to make the party in default compensate for the damages where there is adequate causation between the default in performance of obligation and the damages occurred. Then, this applies to both ordinary damages and special damages, and as for the special damages, the special circumstances shall be taken into account as the basis of determining the question of adequate causation, only if such circumstances were foreseen or foreseeable.

254. However, the origin of the 'theory of adequate causation' was German jurisprudence. The German civil law adopts a principle of restitution, that is, to compensate for all damages where the wrongful act was a cause-in-fact. The theory of adequate causation was developed by the jurists for the purpose of adequately limiting the scope of application of this principle. Contrary to this, Article 416 of the Civil Code of Japan derives itself from one English case in 1854 (*Hadley v. Baxendale*)[143] and adopts from the outset the principle to compensate for only a limited scope of damage (i.e., ordinary damage and special damage).

255. Some jurists, based on the background thus explained, point out that the theory of adequate causation is not relevant to Article 416. Then, some jurists suggest new criteria for calculation of damages which will replace the theory of adequate causation. However, there is no necessity to abandon the theory of

142. STJ (Civil and Criminal Affairs Union) 22 May 1926 Minshu 5-386.
143. *Hadley v. Baxendale*, [1854] 9 Ex. 341; 156 E.R. 145.

adequate causation, which has been widely accepted by case law, and to introduce a new legal concept.

§4. Equitable Limitation of Damages

I. Considering the Pre-existing Special Condition of the Victim

256. Case law holds that Article 722(2) of the Civil Code, the provision on comparative negligence shall be applied *mutatis mutandis*, if it is necessary to mitigate the damages considering the pre-existing special condition of the victim from the viewpoint of fair allocation of damages between the parties. For example, this mitigation may be applied in case the increased damages occur not only by the tortfeasor's act but also by the victims' pre-existing disease or his mental condition.[144] Therefore, the tortfeasor may claim reduction in the amount of increased damages, on the ground of any special physical or mental condition of the victim which existed before the tort was committed.

257. However, case law tends not to apply this provision *mutatis mutandis*, in case the increased damages occur by the victim's unusual body characteristic in comparison with that of reasonable person, or in case such damages occur by the victim's mental condition but his personal character was considered as normal. In one case where the victim has unusual long neck and it was considered as a factor to increasing damages, the Supreme Court states that mitigation of damages shall not be applied, as long such body characteristic is not considered as a disease.[145] In another case where the worker committed suicide by hanging from depression due to long hours of work, the Supreme Court states that, as long as the personal character of the worker is assumed to be normal, it is not able to consider such character as his mental condition letting him suicide, and therefore, it is not able to mitigate damages by applying Article 722(2) *mutatis mutandis*.[146]

II. Considering the Benefit and Loss Counterbalance

258. Although there is no explicit provision in the Civil Code setting forth the benefit and loss counterbalance, it is permissible to do so from the standpoint of fair allocation of damages. For example, in calculating the income losses caused by the death of a person, some items of expenses shall be deducted. Requirement for this deduction is that such loss and benefit shall be of the same nature in terms of legal aspects. Therefore, living expenses are subject to benefit and loss counterbalance, because living expenses would have been incurred if the deceased survived.[147] To

144. See, e.g., SCJ 21 Apr. 1988 Minshu 42-4-243; SCJ 25 Jun. 1992 Minshu 46-4-400.
145. SCJ 29 Oct. 1996 Minshu 50-9-2474.
146. SCJ 24 Mar. 2000 Minshu 54-3-1155.
147. See, e.g., SCJ 24 Jun. 1964 Minshu 18-5-874; SCJ 17 Dec. 1968 Hanji 546-62; SCJ 8 Oct. 1981 Hanji 1023-47.

the contrary, income losses of children who died and childcare expenses to be borne by parents are not of the same nature and cannot be counterbalanced.[148]

259. Life insurance benefits or fire insurance benefits are not subject to the counterbalancing, as they are consideration for the payment of the insurance premiums.[149] However, automobile insurance benefits, both compulsory and voluntary, are subject to the counterbalancing.[150] Among the various social insurance,[151] worker's accident insurance is subject to the counterbalancing in case of personal injury,[152] but not in case of personal death where the heir of worker has received such insurance.[153] Also, survivor's pension as a part of annuity insurance is subject to the counterbalancing, to the extent that was settled to receive,[154] with the inheritance rights to demand pecuniary loss (lost profits) of the deceased by his or her heirs.[155]

260. In case both counterbalancing and comparative negligence are applied in the same case, case law holds that comparative negligence shall be applied first, and then counterbalancing shall be made.[156]

§5. Methods of Payment

261. The Civil Code does not expressly provide for the method of compensation of damages. There are two methods, i.e., 'lump-sum payment method' and 'installment payment method'. The Supreme Court does not allow the lump sum payment method in general,[157] but the recent lower court precedents are inclined to allow the instalment payment method, limited to the future nursing care costs.[158]

148. See, e.g., SCJ 24 Jun. 1964 Minshu 18-5-874; SCJ 20 Oct. 1978 Minshu 32-7-1500.
149. See, e.g., SCJ 31 May 1996 Minshu 50-6-1323 (life insurance); SCJ 31 Jan. 1975 Minshu 29-1-68 (fire insurance).
150. For detail of automobile insurance, see Part III, Ch. 1 and Part VI, Ch. 6, s. 1.
151. For detail of social insurance, see Part VI, Ch. 6, s. 2.
152. See, SCJ 15 Oct. 2010 Shumin 235-65.
153. See, e.g., SCJ 27 May 1977 Minshu 31-3-427; SCJ 25 Oct. 1977 Minshu 31-6-836; SCJ 23 Feb. 1996 Minshu 50-2-249.
154. See, SCJ (FB) 24 Mar. 1993 Minshu 47-4-3039.
155. For detail of succession of rights to demand pecuniary and non-pecuniary loss of the deceased, see Part VI, Ch. 4, s. 3.
156. See, e.g., SCJ 18 Dec. 1980 Minshu 34-7-888; SCJ 11 Apr. 1989 Minshu 43.4.209.
157. See SCJ 6 Feb. 1987 Hanji 1232-100.
158. See, e.g., Osaka DCJ 22 Feb. 1993 Hanta 834-161; Tokyo DCJ 10 Dec. 1996 Hanji 1589-81; Osaka DCJ 26 Jun. 1998 Hanta 1001-196; Tokyo DCJ 7 Oct. 2003 Hanta 1172-253; Osaka DCJ 21 Jan. 2004 Hanta 1174-264.

Chapter 4. Personal Injury and Death

§1. Pecuniary Losses

262. As for the pecuniary losses, including both actual losses and lost profits, the formula for calculation of lost profits becomes very crucial issue in case of personal death and injury. In case of personal injury, 'reduction in income' for reasons of hospitalization or outpatient, 'loss of working capacity' for reasons of after-effects, etc., is considered as lost profits of the victim.

263. The basic formula is to calculate the gross income for the victim's work expectancy out of his/her life expectancy, on the basis of his/her income at the time of his/her death or injury. Then, for calculating the amount of income losses,[159] expected future raises in salary may also be taken into account, but on the other hand, interim interest shall be deducted.[160] In case of personal death, it is difficult to calculate lost profits when the victim (the diseased) was a child, woman or foreign worker, etc., because the basis of his or her income at the time of his or her death is unclear.

264. As for the lost profits of child, the Supreme Court held that, for the purpose of calculation of lost profits of child killed in the accident, the amount calculated shall be as objective as possible, based on the materials such as various statistical data and in accordance with empirical rules and good common sense, and that it was not permissible to reject a claim of compensation of lost profits of child merely on the ground that the amount is incalculable.[161]

265. As for the lost profits of woman, case law in Japan has a tendency to find it inevitable that the income losses of women are evaluated lower than that of men. The Supreme Court, in connection with the calculation of income losses of an 11-year old girl killed in the traffic accident, held that the amount shall be calculated on the basis of the average income of salaried women workers, not on the basis of the average income of the whole of salaried workers.[162]

266. As for the lost profits of foreign workers, the Supreme Court, in connection with an illegal foreign worker, held as follows:

> as for the estimated future working hours or period of stay in Japan, the lost profits shall be calculated on the basis of the income in Japan; and, as for the

159. See, SCJ 27 Aug. 1968 Minshu 22-8-1704 (obiter dictum).
160. See, SCJ 14 Jun. 2005 Minshu 59-5-983 (the rate of interim interest shall be based on the 'statutory interest rate' in Art. 404 of the Civil Code, which states 5% per annum.).
161. SCJ 24 Jun. 1964 Minshu 18-5-874.
162. SCJ 9 Jul. 2002 Kominshu 35-4-917.

period after leaving Japan, the income losses shall be calculated on the basis of the income in the destination country (in most cases, his or her home country).[163]

§2. NON-PECUNIARY LOSSES

267. In case of personal injury, if a victim suffers any non-pecuniary loss (i.e., mental loss), such person is entitled to claim 'solatium' for such loss under Article 710 (Compensation for Damages Other than Property) of the Civil Code. It states that:

> Persons liable for damages under the provisions of the preceding Article must also compensate for damages other than those to property, regardless of whether the body, liberty or reputation of others have been infringed, or property rights of others have been infringed.

268. In case of personal death, the next of kin of the victim respectively has the right to claim *solatium* of his/her own. According to Article 711 (Compensation for Damages to Next of Kin) of the Civil Code, 'A person who has taken the life of another must compensate for damages to the father, mother, spouse and children of the victim, even in cases where the property rights of the same have not been infringed.'

There is an issue whether a person other than the victim's next of kin is entitled to the remedy under this provision or not. Case law tends to expand the scope of the 'next of kin'. For example, there is a case that the court held that 'spouse' as referred to in Article 711 of the Civil Code includes a common-law wife, because a common-law wife is deemed to hold quasi-marital status.[164] Another example is that the court held that, in connection with a claim for *solatium* by the 'sister of the victim's husband' (i.e., sister-in-law) who lived with the victim for a long time and had been supported by the victim, the provision of Article 711 of the Civil Code could be analogically applied.[165]

269. Article 711 of the Civil Code entitles the victim's next of kin to claim *solatium* when the victim dies, but according to case law, it is also applicable to the case of the victim's injury. The Supreme Court held that the mother of the victim could claim *solatium* for her daughter's injury on her face.[166]

163. SCJ 28 Jan. 1997 Minshu 51-1-78.
164. See, Osaka DCJ 22 Apr. 1997 Kominshu 30-2-568.
165. See, SCJ 17 Dec. 1974 Minshu 28-10-2040.
166. See, SCJ 5 Aug. 1958 Minshu 12-12-1901.

§3. Succession of Rights to Demand Pecuniary and Non-pecuniary Loss

270. The right to demand compensation of damages for both pecuniary and non-pecuniary losses entitled to the victim extinguishes upon his or her death. However, the Japanese case law upholds that such right to demand compensation of damages can be succeeded to by his or her heirs. Therefore, according to case law and majority of academic, an heir of the victim may exercise the claim for compensation of pecuniary losses of the deceased,[167] as well as the claim for non-pecuniary loss (*solatium*) of the deceased.[168] As a result, such heir is entitled to claim both *solatium* of the deceased and that of his own under Article 711 of the Civil Code.

271. However, there is a criticism against the succession of such rights of the deceased. This view is based on the precondition that 'only the victim has the right to demand compensation for his or her damages and such right extinguishes upon his or her death'. According to this criticism, the issues related to the right to demand compensation of pecuniary losses by the victim (the deceased) shall be reconsidered as an infringement of the surviving family members' benefit for life support. In addition, the issues related to the right to claim *solatium* of the diseased shall not be admitted, because the surviving family members are already entitled to exercise respectively the right to claim *solatium* for his/her own under Article 711 of the Civil Code.

167. See, STJ 25 Mar. 1932 Hyoron 21 Civil Law 261 STJ 27 Dec. 1941 Minshu 20-1479. Cf. STJ 20 Apr. 1920 Minroku 26-553; STJ 16 Feb. 1926 Minshu 5-150; STJ 10 Mar. 1928 Minshu 7-152.
168. See, SCJ (FB) 1 Nov. 1967 Minshu 21-9-2249. Cf. STJ 3 May 1927 Shimbun 3568-5.

Chapter 5. Various Damages (Property)

272. In case there is an infringement against property right, which is considered as an absolute right, tort liability shall be established. See General Introduction, §6 above. Loss which might be included in the scope of damage is 'actual loss' caused to the victim's property. See Part VI, Chapter 2, §5 above.

273. Recently, there is a case where the contractor who built a defective building is liable under tort law by reason of infringement of 'protective interest of residence' for purchaser of the building.[169] See Part II, Chapter 1, §2 above. This case shows that an infringement against protective interest related to property may also be considered as a damage which shall be compensated under tort law.

274. When there is a defect to the product which is moveable and which is manufactured or proceeded, according to Article 3 of the Product Liability Act (1994), 'the manufacturer, etc. shall be liable for damages arising from the infringement of life, body or property of others which is caused by the defect in the delivered product which was manufactured, processed, imported'. See Part III, Chapter 2 above. This is a case where the defective product also causes the extended damages, such as 'the infringement of life, body or property of others', and these damages shall also be compensated under tort law.

169. See SCJ 17 Jun. 2010 Minshu 64-4-1197.

Chapter 6. Interference with Collateral Benefits

§1. Insurance

275. As already mentioned before, one of the three functions of tort law is the 'recovery of damage' for the victim,[170] and it is the most important one. However, even if the injuring party is held liable to compensate for damages, the victim will not be remedied unless the injuring party actually performs compensation of damages to the victim. In addition, even if the injuring party has an intention to pay compensation, the victim will not be remedied as long as the tortfeasor cannot afford it. In conclusion, it is important to secure that the victim will receive compensation of damages, and the most important security measure is the insurance system.

In the case of an automobile accident, for example, a potential injuring party pays insurance premiums to the insurance company, and, if the injuring party causes an accident and causes damages to a third party, the insurance company pays insurance benefit to the victim.[171] As not all automobile owners or drivers cause accidents, the amount of prepaid insurance premiums is substantially lower than the insurance benefits to be paid by the insurance company.

276. There is a potential risk that the insurance system may ruin the preventive function of the tort law. However, measures to address the negative points of the insurance system are implemented, i.e., the policy to reduce the amount of insurance premiums if the insured is free from any accident for a certain period of time; or the policy to increase the amount of insurance premiums if the insured causes an accident.

The above is an example of insurance where the insured is the potential injuring party; however, there are also other types of insurances where the insured is the prospective victim. In case where the injuring party is not held liable for compensation of damages because the injuring party's act does not satisfy the requirement of tort liability, such type of insurance plays a key role for remedy of the victim. On the other hand, in case where the injuring party is held liable and has already compensated the victim for damages, as for the compulsory insurance, the insurance company shall be exempted from its obligation to make payment to the extent of the amount indemnified by it (Article 16(2) of the Automobile Liability Security Act).[172] Then, as for the voluntary insurance in such a case, it shall be subject to the benefit and loss counterbalance from the standpoint of fair allocation of damages so that insurance benefit that exceeds the total amount of damages shall be deducted.[173]

170. For detail of function of tort law, see General Introduction, s. 3.
171. For detail of automobile insurance, see Part III, Ch. 1.
172. For detail of this Act, see Part III, Ch. 1.
173. For detail of the benefit and loss counterbalance, see Part VI, Ch. 3, s. 4.

§2. Social Security

277. In Japan, there are five social insurance systems, which are based on compulsory insurance (mutual aid) system, such as medical insurance, annuity insurance, worker's accident insurance, unemployment insurance and nursing insurance. Among them, medical insurance, annuity insurance, or worker's accident insurance might be related with tort law. That is, in case there is a tortious act, it is necessary to make an adjustment to avoid duplication compensation between the compensation paid by the tortfeasor and the social insurance which the victim received or his or her heirs succeeded. More specifically, this becomes a problem when considering the 'benefit and loss counterbalance' from the viewpoint of equitable limitation of damages. For detail, see Part VI, Chapter 3, §4 above.

Chapter 7. Other Remedies

§1. Restitution for Unjust Enrichment

278. As already explained, the Civil Code allows for victim who was defamed to claim to restore his or her reputation against the tortfeasor (Article 723 of the Civil Code). Similar restoration is also possible in case of infringement of business reputation under the Unfair Competition Prevention Act. See Part VI, Chapter 1 above. With the exceptions above, the primary remedy under tort law is a compensation of damage, which shall be determined with reference to monetary value.

279. Claims under tort and unjust enrichment, have different requirements and effects, but both claims can be coexisted. Related provisions for unjust enrichment in the Civil Code are stated in Articles 703–708, but the basic principle is stated in Article 703 as follows:

> Article 703 (Obligation to Return Unjust Enrichment)
> A person who has benefited (hereinafter in this Chapter referred to as 'beneficiary') from the property or labor of others without legal cause and has thereby caused loss to others shall assume an obligation to return that benefit, to the extent the benefit exists.

280. It is necessary to satisfy the following requirements to claim unjust enrichment, such as: (i) the lack of legal cause, (ii) the existence of benefit on the side of beneficiary, (iii) the existence of loss on the side of others, and (iv) causation between such benefit and loss, which are different in comparison with that in tort.

281. As for the legal effects between unjust enrichment and tort, the different provision regarding the extinctive prescription shall be applied. As already explained in Chapter 1 of Part IV, the period to exercise right to claim compensation for damages in tort is limited to three years under Article 724 of the Civil Code, but a claimed based on unjust enrichment, as well as on contract, is limited to ten years under Article 167(1) of the Civil Code.

§2. Injunctive Relief

282. Injunctive relief may become useful remedy in a situation in which environmental pollution and injury to reputation or privacy is continuing. However, there is no explicit provision for tort law in the Civil Code to approve injunction. On the other hand, in Part II (Property Law) of the Code, injunctive relief is approved in case of infringement of possession rights (Articles 197–200), and these provisions shall be applied mutatis mutandis in case of infringement of ownership rights. Also, in the specific laws related to intellectual property law or competition law, injunction is admitted as one of the primary remedies (Article 100 of the Patent

Act, Article 112 of the Copyright Act, and Article 3 of the Unfair Competition Prevention Act). Therefore, it is necessary to understand the development of case law whether or not injunction may be approved in tort cases.

283. In case of environmental pollution cases, there is a limit to applying injunction found in property law above, because only person who has the real right has the right to exercise it. There are two famous Supreme Court cases related to the injunction against noise pollution, one is due to aircraft taking off and landing from Osaka International Airport,[174] and the other is due to bullet train,[175] but claims for injunction were denied in both cases by taking into account the 'public nature' of airport and bullet train. Another Supreme Court case, which is also related with noise pollution due to national highway,[176] held that claim for injunction is denied, and reasoned that there is a double-standard in determining 'unlawfulness' in the case of claim for damages and claim for injunction, and it must be satisfied the higher standard of unlawfulness in the latter case than that in the former case.

284. However, courts tend to admit injunctive relief in case of infringement for right to person or personality, such as, right of reputation or right of privacy. As for the defamation case, the Supreme Court held the pre-injunction of publication ordered by the trial court had legality on the basis of infringement for reputation on the candidate of election.[177] There is also one Supreme Court case, which held an injunction of publication of novel on the grounds of an infringement of both reputation and privacy for female acquaintance that has been the model of novel therein.[178]

§3. Punitive Damages

285. Punitive damages are not available in Japanese tort law, because tort law has not intended to have function as a penalty or sanction against the tortfeasor. See General Introduction, §3 above. However, it has been discussed whether a *solatium* has such function among case law and academics.

286. Concerning the nature and purpose of *solatium*, some academics, which are majority opinions, only admit function for compensation, but others also admit function for penalty so that they assert that large sum of *solatium* should be imposed in case tortfeasor's act was based on his or her intention, or, at least, the amount of *solatium* should differ in the case of negligence and in the case of intention.

174. SCJ (FB) 16 Dec. 1981 Minshu 35-10-1369.
175. Nagoya DCJ 11 Sep. 1980 Hanji 976-40 (the trial court); Nagoya HCJ 12 Apr. 1985 Hanji 1150-30 (The appeal court).
176. SCJ 7 Jul. 1995 Minshu 49-7-2599.
177. SCJ (FB) 11 Jun. 1986 Minshu 40-4-872.
178. SCJ 24 Sep. 2002 Hanji 1802-60.

287. Case law has consistently taken a position to deny a claim for punitive *solatium*. For example, in case of group bashing murder,[179] in a case of chloroquine injury lawsuit,[180] and in a case of a car accident which the driver already repeated traffic accidents in past, and caused a personal death of 8 years old child at the time of driver's license suspension for the third time,[181] the courts has confirmed the function and purpose of *solatium* is limited to compensation for victims.

288. There is also one Supreme Court case which held that it is not possible to enforce in Japan a foreign judgment by California Supreme Court in the US which ordered the punitive damages to the Japanese company.[182]

179. See, e.g., Nagano DCJ (Matsumoto Division) 4 Dec. 2002 Hanta 1147-245; Kyoto DCJ 25 Nov. 1993 Hanta 853-249.
180. Tokyo DCJ 1 Feb. 1982 Hanji 1044-19 (the trial court); Tokyo HCJ 11 Mar. 1988 Hanji 1271-3 (the appeal court).
181. Kyoto DCJ 9 Oct. 2007 Hanta 1266-262.
182. SCJ 11 Jul. 1997 Minshu 51-6-2573.

Selected Bibliography

§1. The English Translation of the Civil Code and Other Statutes in Japan

Japanese Law Translation Database System, at <http://www.japaneselawtranslation.go.jp/>.

NLIRO (Non-Life Insurance Rating Organization of Japan), Automobile Liability Security Law & Related Cabinet Ordinance, Ministerial Ordinance and Notification (NLIRO, 2005).

§2. Tort Law in General

Hirai Yoshio. 'Japanese Tort Law in Comparative Perspective'. *Japanese Annual of International Law* 33 (1990): 90–94.

Hondius Ewoud (ed.). *Modern Trends in Tort Law: Dutch and Japanese Law Compared.* (The Hauge: Kluwer Law International, 1999).

Oda Hiroshi. *Japanese Law.* (3rd ed., Oxford University Press, 2009): 180–200.

Mitsuru Claire Chino, Noboru Kashiwagi & Ayako Oda. 'Chapter 5 Contract and Tort'. In *Japanese Business Law,* edited by Gerald Paul Mcalinn. (The Netherland: Kluwer Law International, 2007), 204–220.

Ono Shusei. 'The Law of Torts and the Japanese Civil Law (1): Comparative Law and the Civil Code of Japan (III)'. *Hitotsubashi Journal of Law and Politics* 26 (1998): 43–62.

Ono Shusei. 'The Law of Tort and the Japanese Civil Law (2)'. *Hitotsubashi Journal of Law and Politics* 27 (1999): 9–27.

Osaka Eri. 'Reevaluating the Role of the Tort Liability System in Japan'. *Arizona Journal of International and Comparative Law* 26 (2009): 393–426.

Ramseyer J. Mark & Nakazato Minoru. *Japanese Law An Economic Approach* (The University of Chicago Press, 1999): 75–107.

§3. Strict Liability

Luke Nottage. 'Chapter 6 Product Liability and Safety Regulation'. In *Japanese Business Law*, edited by Gerald Paul Mcalinn. (The Netherland: Kluwer Law International, 2007): 221–262.

Selected Bibliography

Matsumoto Tsuneo. 'Recent Developments in the Law of Product Liability in Japan'. *Hitotsubashi Journal of Law and Politics* 25 (1997): 15–28.

Ono Shusei. 'Strict Liability in Japanese Tort Law, Especially Automobile Liability'. *Hitotsubashi Journal of Law and Politics* 28 (2000): 1–16.

§4. CAUSATION

Hayashida Seimei. 'The Necessity for the Rational Basis of Duty-Risk Analysis in Japanese Tort Law: A Comparative Study'. *Utah Law Review* 1981 (1981): 65–90.

Ono Shusei. 'Joint Unlawful Act in Japanese Tort Law'. *Hitotsubashi Journal of Law and Politics* 29 (2001): 15–23.

§5. DAMAGES

Kojima Hideki. 'Calculation of Damages and "Lost Profits" under Japanese Law: A Comparison with German and United States law'. *Journal of Japanese Law (Zeitschrift für Japanisches Recht)* 31 (2011): 223–236.

Leflar Robert. 'Personal Injury Compensation Systems in Japan: Values Advanced and Values Undermined'. *University of Hawai'I Law Review* 15 (1993): 742–756.

Morishima Akio & Malcolm Smith. 'Accident Compensation Schemes in Japan: A Window to the Operation of Law in a Society'. *University of British Columbia Law Review* 20 (1986): 491–533.

Index

The numbers here refer to paragraph numbers.

Index

Index

www.ingramcontent.com/pod-product-compliance
Lightning Source LLC
Chambersburg PA
CBHW071354230926
51846CB00002B/550
* 9 7 8 9 0 4 1 1 6 0 2 0 1 *